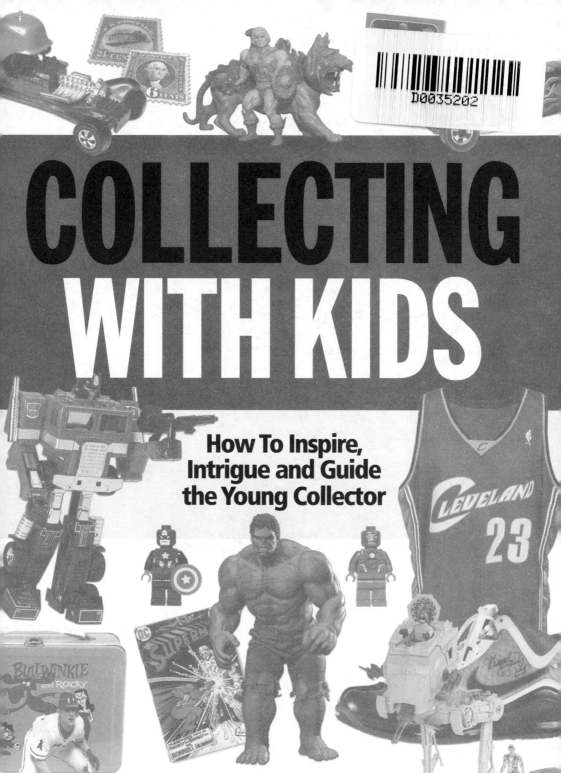

COLLECTING WITH KIDS

How To Inspire, Intrigue and Guide the Young Collector

PAMELA Y. WIGGINS

ADAPTED FROM AUTHOR'S COLUMN IN
THE INTELLIGENT COLLECTOR MAGAZINE

D0035202

Published by

Krause Publications, a division of F+W Media, Inc.
700 East State Street • Iola, WI 54990-0001
715-445-2214 • 888-457-2873
www.krausebooks.com

To order books or other products call toll-free 1-800-258-0929
or visit us online at www.krausebooks.com

ISBN-13: 9781440247460
ISBN-10: 1440247463

Cover Design by Tom Nelsen
Designed by Nicole MacMartin
Edited by Joel Dresang and Mary Sieber

Printed in USA

10 9 8 7 6 5 4 3 2 1

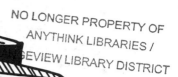

Dedication

To my late mother, Eva Paschal, with whom
I shared many superb collecting adventures.

Acknowledgments

This book wouldn't be possible without the continuing
support of Heritage Auctions and Hector Cantu, who does an
extraordinary job as the editor of *Heritage Magazine for the
Intelligent Collector*, where the original versions of the columns
shared here were first printed.

Many thanks also to Editorial Director Paul Kennedy
and Krause Publications. Paul's support of my work is so
appreciated, as is Krause Publications' dedication to producing
books that educate and inform collectors. I'm forever grateful
for the opportunity to join that worthwhile endeavor.

A hearty round of applause goes to all the numerous
individuals ranging from the collectors to extremely qualified
experts who were interviewed for the columns encapsulated
in this book. I was reminded of all the lively conversations
and exchanges we shared as I updated and prepped this
text. Their willingness to share their knowledge, life lessons,
and enthusiasm for the things they so passionately collect is
appreciated in more ways than they could possibly know.

Lastly, thank you to Jay B. Siegel, my supportive spousal
equivalent. I appreciate him not only for contributing his
photography and editing skills to these articles when I needed
him through the years but for sharing the type of love,
patience, and silliness that keeps me going day in and day out.
I probably could find a way to do what I do without him, but
it wouldn't be nearly as much fun!

Table of Contents

FROM THE AUTHOR

When I look back on my childhood, some of my fondest memories find me by my mother's side. I was a "momma's girl," and where she went, I went. That means when she started hunting antiques in earnest when I was 6 or so, I happily followed along with my curiosity piqued.

Never intent on just observing, I soon began to itch for a collection of my own. I started a little gathering of miniature porcelain animal families and added to it 10 cents at a time at garage sales we scoured together. I found myself drawn to Depression glass at the flea market we frequented, and that led to reading Mom's book on the topic cover to cover. I studied it so often, in fact, that I soon knew all the patterns better than she did. More collections followed, including that set of old glassware I longed for, Snoopy items of all types, and candles shaped like everything from an orange Popsicle to a clever light bulb that actually screwed into a base.

Yes indeed, I caught the collecting "bug" from my mom. She

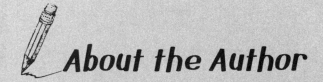

About the Author

With the help of my mom, the collecting badge depicting a treasure chest was the first one I earned as a Junior Girl Scout in the early 1970s. Back then I never imagined I would grow up to obtain a journalism degree from the University of Texas and go on to spend my career educating others about antiques and collectibles. Today, in addition to writing for *Heritage Magazine for The Intelligent Collector*, I can proudly say that I am the author of several books including *Warman's Costume Jewelry*. I am also the antiques expert for About.com, and co-founder of Costume Jewelry Collectors International. Thanks, Mom!

didn't have to do anything special to get me started. She just took me along with her, showed me how much fun she was having, and I wanted in on it, too. Thankfully, I also learned not to be too hard on myself when I made a collecting mistake like those discussed in Part I of this book. She called that "paying for your education" in the antiques biz, and she was right.

Like many young collectors, I took a break through my teen years. That interest in collecting remained dormant until I started thinking about glassware all over again in my mid-20s. Mom didn't need much coaxing to hit the collecting trail with me for a repeat performance, and we started visiting estate sales in the neighborhood where I grew up. There I found glassware, jewelry, and a host of other cool stuff I couldn't resist. Thirty years later, I'm still buying, selling, collecting, and educating others on myriad topics relating to antiques and collectibles.

Writing about the things I discovered while growing up in the middle of an antiquing frenzy, one that eventually led to Mom opening her own business, came naturally to me. I'd learned much more through sheer osmosis as an inquisitive child than I'd realized. Sharing that knowledge with others has been rewarding, exciting, and filled with learning more than I'd ever dreamed when I was tagging along at garage sales and flea markets circa 1970. Mom's been gone since 2007. I still miss calling her to share my latest find. What I'd give for just one more antiquing adventure together!

When I was asked to guide other adults who have the potential for mentoring young collectors, it was not only a thrill for me but a way to honor my mother and the rewarding hobby she shared with me. My regular column called "Kids and Collecting" appears in *Heritage Magazine for The Intelligent Collector,* the periodical published by Heritage Auctions, based in Dallas, Texas. In each issue, I cover a topic designed to inspire adults and give them tools they can use to introduce children to the wonderful world of collecting. Now that you're holding this book, you'll get to learn about all this good stuff, too.

Pamela Y. Wiggins shares a lesson on costume jewelry history with a Central Texas Girl Scout troop.
Photo by Jay B. Siegel

INTRODUCTION

Getting the next generation interested in collecting is a hot topic these days. Collecting clubs are looking at new ways to motivate children. Dealer-related organizations are exploring opportunities to encourage younger members and budding enthusiasts. Editors are seeking articles like those within this book to inspire adult collectors to bring newbies into the fold.

But with so many more things to occupy the time of kids and teens these days, from texting with friends to video games, wandering around a flea market might not be their first choice for entertainment. Of course, how will they know if you don't get them out there and give it a try?

That's what this book is all about. It's designed to give ideas to those who want to pass the collecting legacy along to the next generation. As you peruse the articles compiled here, you'll find that many learning and sharing opportunities are wrapped up in the gift of collecting.

From their collecting mentors, kids learn money management, history related to what they're collecting, and how to be good stewards of the objects in their care. They're guided to communicate about their collections through writing reports and making presentations. They may even find their collecting passion leading to a career. I'm living proof of that, as are many other folks I've interviewed over the years. But most of all, collecting encourages children to have fun because that's the best part of being a kid. Kindling that enjoyment lets you seize the blessing of having a child in your life.

Use these stories as tools for mentoring, inspiring, and helping children to learn and grow. In turn, you may well mold an aficionado who can carry your passion for collecting into the future. They might even teach you a thing or two along the way. At the very least, you'll make some superb memories together that will last a lifetime. No matter how much you value your collections, those shared experiences will be even more valuable.

Kids Who Collect

Share your stories! If you know of a kid who actively collects or an adult-and-child dynamic duo treasure hunting together, email Pamela at aboutantiques@outlook. com. They may end up being featured in her *Heritage Magazine for the Intelligent Collector* column or in one of her About.com articles on collecting topics.

COLLECTING LESSONS 101

Collecting lessons abound for both adults and kiddos. It all starts with discovering cool stuff to research and value, and that amazement whets the appetite for more fabulous finds.

Sometimes, it's about continuing a legacy as well. Everyone hopes the treasures they've gathered will be cherished by others when they're not around anymore. And even if their heirs don't keep every single item they've collected – because that's often difficult to downright impossible – they want them to be educated about the best way to pass the items on to others. Getting a child interested in collecting offers a much better shot at accomplishing these goals.

Another distinct advantage of adults teaching kids the ropes is that the grownups already have made most of the big collecting mistakes. Novices can benefit from the veteran experiences of not noticing an item is broken before paying good money for it or mistaking a reproduction for an authentic old item or overpaying for common pieces. Such fails can be looked upon as "paying for your education" and lessons to pass along because they happen to everyone sooner or later.

A number of adult collectors, some of whom are now earning their living in the antiques and collectibles field, have great ideas and input when it comes to getting kids interested and guiding them successfully. These *are l*essons everyone can learn from, even the old dogs teaching young pups a few new tricks.

A long time ago in a galaxy far, far away Eric Bradley and his son, Patrick, bonded over vintage Star Wars toys.

Chapter 1

Continuing the Collecting Legacy

You've worked for years amassing a formidable collection. Ever wonder what will happen when all those prized possessions pass on to the next generation? Will the objects you cherish be appreciated? Will your entire collection be sold for far less than it's worth?

Questions like these lead some individuals to liquidate lifelong collections when family members show no interest in holding onto them. Other collectors hold out for a change of heart. But is there really anything you can do to increase your odds of developing a budding enthusiast who will continue your legacy?

For many avid collectors, it's merely a matter of starting their children and grandchildren off young and watching the collecting "bug" travel from generation to generation with relative ease. "From the time she was able to walk, she'd go shopping in stores, yard sales and flea markets with me," remarked Victoria Douglass, of New Jersey, about her daughter, Nikole. "This is how I started with my mother and grandmother, too," Douglass said.

"My daughter attaches a memory and is interested in the past of an item. She's curious about who owned it and the time period it's from." Over the years, Douglass found that encouraging her daughter's curiosity helped to develop

The Millennium Falcon LEGO Set in box is a collector's dream, worth as much as $4,500.
Courtesy Eric Bradley

The Star Wars Imperial Shuttle, shown with cool action figures, was introduced in late 1984.

a collecting instinct she sustained over time, and it's a hobby this duo has shared for many years. "Nikole has a great eye and calls me when she's found something that reminds her of me," Douglass said, with a hint of pride.

Other collectors find instilling the collecting sense to be more difficult, but they're making the effort nonetheless. Rita Lynn, of California, wasn't always greeted with enthusiasm when her daughter, Alexandra, was young.

Lynn shared that her daughter actually hated it when they came across antique stores because Alexandra knew her mother would go in and wander the aisles aimlessly. Lynn dealt with it by buying her daughter things so she would partake in the hunt, although Alexandra showed much more interest in collecting beach glass and polished rocks than items found in antique

Some collectibles experts see flea markets as the best child-friendly shopping destinations.

Kid-Friendly Shopping Destinations

While well-behaved children are welcome almost everywhere antiques and collectibles are sold, including antique malls and estate sales, some venues are just more kid-friendly than others. When just getting started to introduce a kid to collecting, consider these shopping spots:

Garage and Yard Sales – Known as "tag" sales in some parts of the United States, garage and yard sales are casual enough to accommodate shoppers of all ages. They often include toys, games, and books among other items that will interest youngsters, and the prices are budget-friendly. It's important to teach little ones to be respectful

shops. And yes, with some encouragement, those everyone-can-do-it collecting interests can lead to greater aspirations, too.

About.com's former collectibles expert, Barb Crews, suggested, "In this crazy, busy world, sometimes it's as easy as just doing it together. Looking for state quarters, trading pins at Disney World, doing squished pennies at tourist locations – these are all ways to get interested in collecting, and one collection always leads to another."

Eric Bradley, a public relations associate for Heritage Auctions and author of several books, including *Mantiques: A Manly Guide to Cool Stuff*, found a common interest with his son, Patrick, when he began showing his own collections to

of the property of others, and these types of sales are a great place to start.

Flea Markets – Some collectibles experts see flea markets as the best child-friendly shopping destinations out there. The vendors have already picked the local garage sales and offer a wide range of collectibles in all price ranges. This is a no-frills setting for shopping, which is perfect for kids learning and exploring with their adult mentors.

Thrift Stores – It takes more diligence to find collectibles at thrift stores these days, but it is possible. Tackling thrift store shopping means frequent visits to see what's new. This type of shopping isn't for everyone, but with some guidance and patience, kids can come away with an occasional treasure – and their grown-up buddies can, too.

Patrick a number of years ago.

"Patrick's Spider-Man collection was influenced by the movies and my own collection of comic books and '80s superhero toys I saved," Bradley said. "I waited until he was 5 to share these things with him, and it sparked his curiosity." Patrick has been known to collect Star Wars as well, mainly focusing on vintage items his dad remembers from his youth, after amassing a nice collection of modern action figures, posters, and LEGO themed play sets.

Bradley also shared the task of cultivating his young son's interests with a friend. "Another heavy influence was a relationship he developed with Lou Kuritzky, a Florida doctor, educator and dealer/collector of antique bookends. Lou and I met at an Atlantique City show and started talking about my son's collection. He offered to strike up pen pal correspondence with Patrick as a way to develop a new collector. Every few months or so, Lou sent Patrick a box of Spider-Man items. Likewise, Patrick has gone out of his way to notice bookends Lou might find interesting and helped him start a collection of

All things LEGO are hot, including this LEGO Ghostbusters Ecto–1, with accompanying minifigures.

miniature bookends."

Bradley added, "I guess when it comes to collecting, it may 'take a village' to get the next generation interested." And with children becoming more and more computer savvy at earlier ages, kids find connecting to the global collecting network easier than ever to accomplish.

"The Internet is a perfect way to learn more about items – from history to availability, and of course, values – to make sure one doesn't overpay at a collectibles show or flea market," Crews noted. "With a digital camera, children can also easily take pictures of their collection and put them on the computer using a picture-sharing program like Flickr."

Crews values teaching children how to shop online, too, including time she spent tutoring her grandson. "He has been an avid eBay browser since he was about 2 years old. We would spend 'quality time' looking at listings of Elmo in the beginning, and then moving on to vintage LEGO and vintage Star Wars."

Bradley agrees that the shopping aspect ranks high in training young collectors, and he lets his children surf online auctions and other collectibles websites as well. But when it comes to getting serious about amassing collections, he feels there's nothing like a good old-fashioned flea market for family outings.

"Flea markets are about the most

A keen eye could spot a flea– market treasure like R2-D2.

The Millennium Falcon,
made famous by Han Solo,
was introduced in 1979.

child-friendly antique and collectible shopping environment ever," Bradley said. "The informal setting is perfect for children. Kids are amazed at the quantity of items for sale at flea markets, and the constant variety keeps their attention. Sometimes, our kids will walk through an entire flea market several times and find something new on each trip.

"Children should never be sent around unsupervised, however," Bradley added. Managing the online collecting activity of children and their interaction with adult collectors in all instances also makes good sense.

Beyond the all-important safety coaching, there are a number of other horizon-expanding lessons children have the opportunity to learn through collecting. "We don't give our kids money to spend at the flea markets," Bradley said. "Instead, they are encouraged to earn money by selling toys they are no longer interested in. They can use those proceeds to buy whatever they like, but our goal is to show them collecting is not synonymous with hoarding. We also want to teach them about the concept of

trading up and that getting rid of things can be an important aspect of collecting."

Douglass noted several lessons her children learned through collecting as well: developing research skills, comparing objects from the past to modern inventions, and practicing patience when searching for specific items. Learning to respect the property of others and care for a collection to maintain its value also rank high on the list of helpful lessons gleaned through collecting as a family.

Of course, there are going to be times when no amount of shopping, surfing, educating or cajoling will spark an interest. While Douglass witnessed Nikole pursuing her own collecting interests effortlessly, her son, Jereme, also went along on their antiquing adventures but never really caught the bug. "He always liked antiques, and he enjoys specific pieces he has from me," Douglass said. "He just doesn't like the clutter, as he calls it. I guess his interest in tennis just took first place over collecting."

Crews has advice for collectors who may face similar circumstances and wonder what will become of their possessions in the future: "Even if they don't want to keep the collection, it's important for the parent to pass along the history and value of a collection for when it does ultimately get disbursed. And as far as I'm concerned, that's fine, as long as they don't sell everything I have for a quarter each at a garage sale when I'm gone. But if they do, they're the ones losing out, and I make sure they know it!"

"Researching the proper way to store and display any type of collection is paramount to preserving treasured items and their values."
— Elyse Luray

Chapter 2

KEEP THEM FROM LEARNING "THE HARD WAY"

Elyse Luray

Collecting mistakes – overlooking critical flaws, buying fakes, overpaying for things that turn out to be incredibly common, along with a host of other concerns for collectors – inevitably happen, if you enjoy the hobby long enough. Collectors on all levels learn "the hard way," and that's all the more reason to mentor young collectors in your life so they can experience less disappointment and more fun.

"A lot of buying done by kids is accomplished online today, so you're using what's presented rather than touching and seeing. In some ways, there's a higher risk" of making a buying mistake, said Elyse Luray, a collectibles expert who appeared on the

---

Elyse Luray, a collectibles expert who appeared on the PBS television series "History Detectives" and Syfy's "Collector Intervention".

PBS television series "History Detectives" and Syfy's "Collector Intervention". It's important to teach children to examine photos for flaws, ask questions about condition issues common to items they're familiar with and assess the seller's reputation, along with return policies, before making a purchase online. Setting spending limits is also important.

"They compete online to buy things they like, so it's important that they learn to have a ceiling," just as an adult collector would when bidding in an auction to avoid overpaying,

Luray said. "My older son collects sneakers, and there's a big secondary market for that these days. There's actually a consignment store in Manhattan that specializes in collectible sneakers." Whether visiting a brick-and-mortar store or shopping online, Luray guides her son to research "comparables" before making a purchase.

Appraisers like Luray use comparables, or documented sold items exactly like the one being valued, to assess current pricing information. If you can't find one exactly like the item being sold,

Fifteen pairs of NBA stars'
game used and signed
sneakers from the 1990s.
Courtesy of Heritage Auctions,
ha.com

look for one as close as possible, always remembering to consider condition. Comparables are usually gleaned from auction records, information provided by dealers and personal experience, if the appraiser is closely familiar with the type of item being evaluated. Adult collectors can help kids research their own comparables using resources like completed-item searches on eBay.com, searching Heritage Auction records for selling prices at HA.com or subscribing to a valuation service, like WorthPoint.com (for a monthly fee).

Sometimes, doing a bit of dissuading is helpful to children

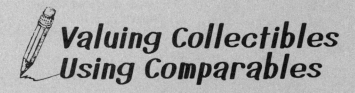

Valuing Collectibles Using Comparables

Valuing collectibles – whether before, during or after a collecting expedition – is one of the most important areas where kids need the guidance of adults. Appraisers use comparables, or documented sold items exactly like the ones being valued, to assess current pricing information. You can, too. If you can't find a piece exactly like the item being sold, look for one as close as possible. Always take condition into consideration.

Comparables are usually gleaned from auction records, information provided by dealers, and personal experience, if you're closely familiar with the type of item being evaluated. In addition to many print-based reference guides like *Antique Trader Antiques & Collectibles Price*

as well. For example, Luray strongly discourages buying limited editions for a collection.

"It's always best to buy originals, whether you're purchasing comic books or movie posters or whatever your interest is," Luray said. She noted that many limited editions are targeted toward younger collectors since they often coincide with current movie trends. Because these items are made to be saved and collected, they rarely increase in value. In fact, in most instances, they drastically decrease in worth over time. Saving hard-earned

Guide by Eric Bradley (Krause Publications), these online resources can help with valuation tasks:

eBay.com Completed Item Searches – Through the Advanced Search feature at eBay, you can search for both asking prices and sold item final values.

HA.com – From sports cards to space memorabilia to comic book art, all types of auction listings can be found on the Heritage Auctions website.

WatchCount.com – Another resource for looking up completed eBay auctions that also shows the final values for listings where the "make an offer" feature was used in a transaction. This can be very helpful since that information is not available via eBay's completed item listings.

WorthPoint.com – For a fee, with a free trial period available, users can access a database of more than 300 million sold item listings. Articles by collectibles experts are also available as research tools on the site.

allowance dollars to buy the best original, older item a child can afford makes much more sense in the long run.

Rob Rosen, who frequently evaluates sports collectibles for Heritage Auctions, also finds that buying from less-than-reputable sellers can be a big problem and one of the mistakes he runs across quite often. But it's also a mistake that can easily be avoided. "Ask around for recommendations from other collectors," Rosen advised. "Another great way to meet reputable sellers is to go to trade shows where everything from coins to comics are offered for sale."

Buying from conscientious dealers means that items like coins and some sports memorabilia are authenticated and graded properly by a third party, which should also be an agency with good standing among collectors. This minimizes the chance of buying a fake or an item in poor condition. Rosen also suggests that adults guide young collectors in "staying on top of the subject matter" being collected by doing online research, reading trade magazines and following trends to avoid paying too much – as well as selling for too little, another collecting mistake.

So, you can work toward always buying top quality at the right price, but what about after a child adds an item to a collection? One of the most common mistakes made by collectors also happens to be one of the most avoidable.

"In a word, storage," Luray advised. "Not caring for the pieces by taking things like humidity and dust into consideration, storing in attics and garages, is a big problem." In every episode of her television series "Collector Intervention," where she helped adults get their collections back in good order, storage proved to be a major issue. In some instances, it had a grave impact on the future value of pieces in a collection. Researching the proper way to store and display any type of collection is paramount to preserving treasured

Children learn to enjoy what they collect by displaying their treasures.

items and their values.

Rosen sees this as an issue as well, adding that displaying collections away from direct sunlight is also important. He's seen his share of autographs that have faded when they were mounted and displayed improperly. He urges collectors to "go to a framer who frequently deals with collectibles to make sure they use the right type of glass" and other materials.

Documenting a collection is another area where folks of all ages often fall short. Whether using a computerized spreadsheet the child can access or a spiral notebook, record the date each item was acquired, where it was purchased, any known facts about the piece to confirm provenance, how much was paid and the condition at the time of purchase. Then, if the child decides to sell an item to upgrade his or her collection or wants to avoid buying a duplicate of an item in storage, an easily accessible record is available as a memory jogger.

A clear acrylic display case keeps collectibles safe.

Another big question that often comes up when talking about preventing collecting mistakes: Should children be allowed to play with their collections? According to Luray, the answer is emphatically "no."

"I might not be too popular for saying that, but I don't believe that items in a collection are toys. I think you should buy specific toys to play with but preserve a collection," Luray said.

Luray learned this lesson well when she walked into her 4-year-old son's bedroom one day to find him throwing an autographed Joe DiMaggio baseball back and forth with a friend. "From that time on, all the collectibles in our house went into display boxes."

But even so, Luray added, "There's no point to amass a collection if you can't enjoy it." She earnestly encourages adults to teach children how to properly display items they collect or receive as gifts so they can be enjoyed and shared with others. And, of course, sharing good times together pursuing a collecting hobby is never a mistake.

"The most important thing is creating memories," Luray said. "What they remember about doing those things together is just as valuable as the collection made in the process."

Various collectibles are securely stored but easily viewed in a cabinet with glass sides and door.

"I think if I'd known then what I know now, I would have taken better care of my things while encouraging all my friends' mothers to throw theirs out."
— Joe Fay

Chapter 3

WHAT THEY KNOW NOW – EXPERTS SHARE COLLECTING LESSONS

Many experts working in the field of antiques and collectibles today started collecting at a young age. Not only are they still appreciating and amassing treasures after all these years, but they earn their living surrounded by fascinating historical memorabilia and collectibles they appreciate even more as adults.

These seasoned pros have learned valuable lessons along their collecting journeys. Looking back, three veteran collectors provide some great suggestions for giving children a leg up by reflecting on how they got started and "what they wish they knew then."

Michael Riley

Michael Riley's interests have run the gamut when it comes to history and popular culture. It all started at 8 when his curiosity was piqued after his Uncle George gave him a bag of coins he'd gathered in travels. Riley acquired some inexpensive folders to catalog them and added to the collection

Riley

Michael Riley is chief cataloger and historian for Heritage Auctions' Americana division.

simply by pilfering through pocket change. He even turned
his dollar-a-week allowance into a collection, quite literally, by
asking for silver dollars instead of bills when he visited the bank
with his parents.

Like any dedicated collector, Riley didn't stop there. Nearly
everything he took an interest in became a collection, from
baseball and football cards depicting members of his favorite
teams to comic books he loved to read. "I have that gene,
apparently," he said about his propensity to collect.

His Uncle George also gave him a box of fascinating old
postcards from the early 1900s that led to a stamp collection.
Another beloved Uncle, Will, who was a professor and a friend
of Dwight D. Eisenhower, would send along books and historical
papers he thought his nephew might find interesting. "These
things instilled my love of history," Riley recalled.

Hopeful pins used in the 1948 effort to draft Dwight D. Eisenhower as a presidential candidate.
Courtesy of Heritage Auctions, ha.com

There are not sure bets, but The Beatles are considered the blue-chip stock of collecting.

Of course, Riley's collecting approach now is different than it was way back when. "I've learned they were right when they say 'don't clean your coins,'" Riley said. "And don't put your baseball cards in the spokes of your bicycle tires with a clothespin so they make a fun noise. I did that, too!"

He also knows now that gluing stamps into albums isn't a good idea, nor is removing them from old postcards, since collectors want cards to be as complete as possible. Luckily, nothing extremely valuable was destroyed or damaged as he pursued his hobbies as a youngster, but Riley acknowledges that the results of his missteps could have been disastrous.

"Condition is everything to collectors," he shared. He suggests guiding kids to collect cautiously so they can preserve the objects they're amassing.

And who knows? Some of the things youngsters find interesting today may end up in the hands of an auction cataloger with a love of history like Riley at some point. As the chief cataloger and historian for Heritage Auctions' Americana division, he specializes in space memorabilia now but has done catalog work with comics and all types of celebrity, music and entertainment memorabilia since he joined the auction house in 2004.

In fact, as an avid Beatles fan, Riley was thrilled by an item he was privy to handle: a wall autographed by all four Beatles from the set of the Ed Sullivan Show dating to 1964. Not bad for a boy who got his start sorting through a bag of hand-me-down coins.

The Beatles School Bag made homework hip in 1964. Almost.

A Yellow Submarine alarm clock was a ringing success in 1968.

The Beatles Disk-Go-Case record carrier, 1966.

Marsha Dixey

Lots of kids love horses. But Marsha Dixey, who's production manager in Heritage Auctions' Americana division and serves on the collectibles panel for *Country Living* magazine, took her equine fondness in a different direction by transforming it into a collection at the young age of 6.

Dixey

She gathered model horses by Hartland, including Roy Rogers' Trigger and Dale Evans' Buttermilk, and a number of other toy examples. She also added to her collection of porcelain and glass horses that she won at summertime carnivals. By the time she put that collection to bed, her stable included 80 different horse examples. That was quite a feat for a kid working with a small allowance for a budget.

Civil War–era snare drum and drum sticks.

As it turns out, Dixey's passion for history and memorabilia and the collecting of these items runs in her family. "I have to blame my grandparents," Dixey said. "One of my grandmothers was a member of Daughters of the

Marsha Dixey, production manager in Heritage Auctions' Americana division and member of the collectibles panel for Country Living magazine.

Collectible horses including some Hartland models.
Courtesy of Milestone Auctions, www.milestoneauctions.com

American Revolution, and she was a Daughter of the Confederacy. All my grandparents were very proud of their heritage, and they taught me to appreciate the rich history that surrounded us."

Dixey found herself trekking along with her grandparents to famed historical sites like Williamsburg and Jamestown and many Civil War battlegrounds where her grandfather would look for artifacts. She also accompanied them to museums steeped in regional history, and, of course, they frequented antique shops while they were out together. Drawn to mid-1800s objects, she later amassed collections of American primitive furniture and quilts to use in her home. "I was an early recycler," Dixey said.

Her interest in history later led Dixey to collect political memorabilia, suffragette items, and other social history pieces as well. She learned how important history is to what and where we are today as a society – and personally, too. As she matured,

Dixey also found that value isn't the only thing that matters to a collector. She realized how important it is to hang on to things you really love the most, regardless of how much they're worth.

Dixey suggests helping kids with a propensity for collecting learn all they can about their topics of interest. When her son was young, she took him to sports memorabilia shows and imparted lessons on fakes, value levels, and how to use his money wisely. "You can really teach some important economic lessons through collecting," she noted.

Dixey also encouraged her son to read, at a time when he was less than interested, by introducing him to Beckett's publications. He gladly pored over the issues, reading articles to research how to find values for his football and basketball cards. Though their collecting passions were vastly different, Dixey and her son enjoyed all the time they spent together nurturing his interests. She looks back on those times fondly.

Through her job at Heritage, Dixey delves into what she loves most as she works with varied historical memorabilia. She's

1986–'87 Fleer Michael Jordan Chicago Bulls basketball card.

examined some really fascinating photographs and documents, but one really stands out.

Buried deep inside a nice but rather unexciting book of historical memorabilia dating to the Civil War era, Dixey discovered an original wanted poster for John Wilkes Booth. It was in great condition and worth about $45,000. "It was like a lightning bolt hit me when I carefully unfolded that paper," Dixey remembered. That kind of thrill never gets old for this expert who began simply by tagging along with her grandparents.

Joe Fay

Joe Fay, a respected rare books expert, began his first collection in elementary school. He found himself drawn to comic books featuring film characters like Indiana Jones and those from Star Wars. He went on to collect varied items ranging from giant foam fingers and Mr. Potato Head toys to Stephen King books and horror movie posters. He's a true pop culture aficionado who counts as one of his personal career highs the opportunity to handle the first book Stephen King ever autographed.

Fay

Unlike most kids, though, Fay learned early on about the importance of storing collectibles properly to keep them from deteriorating. He used acid-free storage supplies, including backing boards, to keep his comic books in nice shape for future reading. He also learned that if movie posters were originally folded or rolled, it was best to store them in the same manner using acid-free materials. He continues to approach his

Expert Joe Fay has a voracious appetite for rare books.

collecting interests with the same type of exacting care.

One thing Fay didn't take into consideration back then, however, was value. He collected for sheer enjoyment, and there's absolutely nothing wrong with that. Sometimes, though, he wishes he'd known to consult a few comic value guides. He feels that paying more attention to older comics by Marvel and other big names to augment his collection would have been a good investment. He also wishes that he hadn't played with his Star Wars toys quite so hard back then, knowing how much some of them can be worth today.

"It's the scarcity of some of these things that makes them valuable," Fay said. "I think if I'd known then what I know now, I would have taken better care of my things while encouraging all my friends' mothers to throw theirs out."

Now Fay's the father of twin girls and hopes they will share his love for the hobby in the future. When they do, he'll encourage them to collect something they're passionate about. He also plans to guide them toward the right expert contacts and references so that they can learn to collect smartly, taking both conservation and future value into consideration.

Most any child can benefit from the lessons adult collectors have to share. Thinking about what you know now that you wish you'd known then can be a great help in imparting valuable tips with the young collecting buddy in your life.

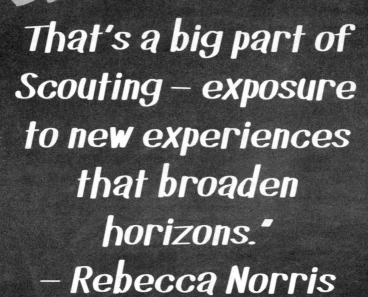

> "That's a big part of Scouting — exposure to new experiences that broaden horizons."
> — Rebecca Norris

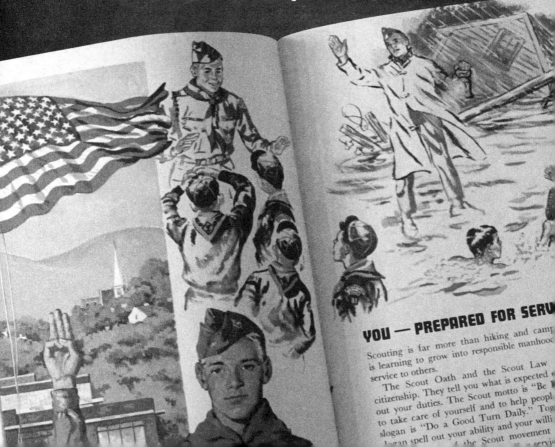

YOU — PREPARED FOR SERV

Scouting is far more than hiking and camp is learning to grow into responsible manhoo service to others.

The Scout Oath and the Scout Law citizenship. They tell you what is expected out your duties. The Scout motto is "Be to take care of yourself and to help peopl slogan is "Do a Good Turn Daily." To logan spell out your ability and your will

Chapter 4

SCOUTING FOR COLLECTORS – EARNING BADGES WHILE BUILDING COLLECTIONS

Scouting for ways to introduce collecting to the next generation? It may be as easy as locating an eager Boy Scout or Girl Scout.

Offer your child, grandchild, or even a neighbor the chance to earn a merit badge by introducing them to collecting, and you just might make an impression to last a lifetime. American scouting branches for boys and girls offer a number of merit badges relating to collecting.

Collecting Badges for Boy Scouts

Getting boys interested in obtaining the general collecting badge offered through Boy Scouts of America shouldn't be much of a task since there's an inherent draw to things they hold an interest in, like sports memorabilia, comic books, and a host of other collectibles. But there are ways to take a Scout's interest in collectibles a step further.

Many helpful resources are available, from special folders dedicated to Boy Scout coin collections to brochures that help budding young coin and stamp

Two vintage Boy Scout medals in original cases.
Courtesy of Omega Auction Corp., www.omegaauctioncorp.com

enthusiasts navigate the requirements for obtaining a badge. Money.org, the American Numismatic Association's website, provides guidance in this area with an introduction to materials available through local Boy Scout Council offices. Some Boy Scout Councils even have expert counselors who assist children pursuing these badges.

"Stamp collecting started early on can lead to a lifetime hobby, and it doesn't have to be expensive, especially

Two cast iron still banks, one with a scout holding an American flag and one holding a Boy Scout Camp flag.
Courtesy of Rich Penn Auctions, www.richpennauctions.com

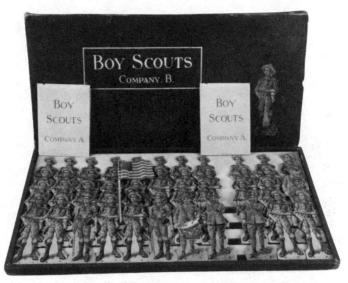

Boy Scouts Company B with 44 paper litho figures on wooden bases in the original box.
Courtesy of Morphy Auctions, morphyauctions.com

Vintage Boy Scout uniform with beret, gloves, socks and more in a May Co. box.
Courtesy of Milestone Auctions, www.milestoneauctions.com

Early Boy Scout items including two canteens, two belts, and a lunch pail.
Courtesy of Milestone Auctions, www. milestoneauctions. com

Kids learn geography and history by collecting stamps.

There are endless options for collecting pursuits that interest girls, such as women's fashion accessories and dolls from around the world.
Courtesy of Morphy Auctions, morphyauctions.com, and Premier Auction Galleries, www.pag4u.com

An assortment of Boy Scout patches.
Courtesy of Pioneer Auction Gallery, www.pioneerantiqueauction.com

when focusing on postally used stamps from around the world," said Joseph Bloom, of North Carolina, who began assisting Boy Scouts as a stamp collecting counselor decades ago.

Many boys tend to start a collection on their own and then seek out a mentor to verify they've completed the requirements for a merit badge. Bloom believes the best approach, however, is to introduce a child to collecting and then guide them through the learning process.

"I've found earning a collecting badge works best when kids come to you as they first start out so you can guide them through the ins and outs," Bloom said. He believes an experienced adult can help a child avoid pitfalls novice collectors are bound to encounter and sidestep bad habits so they won't have to be corrected down the line.

Those encouraging coin collecting...

... will find the American Numismatic Association's "Hints for completing the requirements for the Boy Scout Coin Collecting Merit Badge" particularly useful. Go to Money.org and find the Discover section at the top of the site. Click on the "Scouts" link.

Collecting-Related Badges for Girl Scouts

Earning collecting badges isn't as easy for Girl Scouts as it used to be. For years, young women could garner a general collecting badge, but that's no longer an option. As an alternative, once a year girls now can earn a "Make Your Own" badge. Having a mentor who shares a common interest assist in turning that into a collecting-related badge will help a youngster deepen her appreciation for collectibles.

There are endless options for collecting pursuits that interest girls, like items relating to favorite sports, toys from around the globe, or even fashion history that includes learning about antique jewelry. Making a presentation about a collection can help an entire troop learn about cultural history or the artistry of design and provide an introduction to the fun of hunting and gathering unique collections.

"When my daughter was learning about vintage costume jewelry through the presentation to her troop, I think she got a really good feel for how styles changed through the decades and what influenced those changes from a historical perspective. She also realized that what's old is new again," said Rebecca Norris, of Texas, recalling a Girl Scout meeting held in her home. "All the girls came to understand that styles

Girl Scout badge sash, circa 1960s, Santa Anita Council, with a variety of circular patches and three star pins.
Courtesy of Morphy Auctions, morphyauctions.com

they think are cool today aren't all that much different from the things their grandmothers wore in the '60s and '70s."

But the lessons learned extended beyond the specific collection being shared. "They discovered there are books on collectibles they can study for more information on collecting, and they came away feeling like they could start their own collections, too," Norris said. "If they don't get that type of experience through their own parents and grandparents, then having a guest share with them really opens their eyes to new possibilities. That's a big part of Scouting – exposure to new experiences that broaden horizons."

Life Lessons Learned Through Collecting

The chance to introduce a child to collecting through Scouting is, of course, about more than merely decorating a uniform with colorfully embroidered patches. While children usually don't recognize life lessons as they're happening, a sage collector understands that speaking to a scout troop about a collection or nurturing an individual child helps them grow in ways that extend beyond merely amassing a bunch of stuff.

"As an example, earning a stamp collecting badge is extremely educational. Kids find out about geography and history through collecting stamps," Bloom said. "Beyond that, they have to learn

Vintage Girl Scout uniform.
Courtesy of Main Street Mining Co. Auctions, www.mainstreetminingco.com

55

to stay organized, and pay attention to detail when carefully placing their stamps in an album. It's not all work, though. This kind of learning's also a lot of fun."

As children approach their collection of choice, Bloom also emphasized that they learn about using tools required to research their collectibles, caring for their collections, and discovering the background associated with their hobby as well as the potential value of the collection. When interests and skills are developed early, there's a good chance the passion for collecting will continue to grow.

Rewards for the Mentor

Helping a scout or troop is also a great opportunity to give back. Adults who mentor Scout troops or packs provide a community service, and the leaders of these groups very much appreciate the assistance.

Since collectors gain so much enjoyment from their pastime, they often find sharing their enthusiasm with others to be a rewarding extension of the hobby. Of course, the kids they're working with do learn about an interesting topic in the process. But as mentors, collectors often glean as much or more from the experience as the children they're helping.

"As long as there is a single boy out there in my area who is interested in earning his stamp collecting merit badge, I will continue to serve," Bloom said in a Linns.com article. "There is great reward from working one-on-

Terri Lee doll from the 1950s wearing the original Girl Scout outfit.
Courtesy of Stephenson's Auction, www.stephensonsauction.com

Rebecca Norris with her daughter Brittany learning about jewelry collecting at a Girl Scout meeting.
Photo by Jay B. Siegel

one with a potential lifelong stamp collecting enthusiast."

Ready to inspire a young Scout yourself? If you don't have a built-in family-and-friends connection, talk to your local Boy or Girl Scout council office for ideas on how you can help a pack or troop in your area as an expert counselor or meeting guest.

DECIDING WHAT TO COLLECT

It's a big world out there when it comes to honing in on what to collect. It's up to grown-up mentors guiding youngsters to help them narrow their focus and put together a thoughtful collection. Sometimes it's easy if a kid is drawn to something like action figures, or they're already picking up sports cards related to a favorite team. Seedling collections can already be growing, and all you have to do is recognize and encourage it.

Other times it takes looking at everyday objects as potential collectibles. In fact, you'll find that many of the experts started their lifelong collecting pursuits and rewarding careers simply by sifting through pocket change or picking up pretty rocks to build a collection when they were young.

If nothing takes root inherently and the child is mature enough, try shopping with your little buddy at your favorite antiques mall or taking him to a flea market. Even thrift stores can do the trick. Note what they're interested in as you browse together. What captures their interest and piques their curiosity? Odds are, what they're meant to collect will come into focus as you simply enjoy your time together.

So, as you peruse the upcoming chapters, keep in mind that collecting is an organic hobby, especially when guiding kids. It grows along with children as they mature, explore and discover new things. The genres covered here are merely suggested collecting categories, and each child will be drawn naturally to something different. Glean knowledge from experts in specific fields knowing that where you start collecting as kids may not be where you end up. That's all part of the exciting journey you're embarking upon together.

"

...the most important thing in this case is that collecting action figures should be a fun thing that parents and kids can do together."
— Bobbi Boyd

Chapter 5

ACTION FIGURES – TRANSFORMING TOYS INTO A COOL COLLECTION

Sometimes helping a child start a collection can be pretty darn simple. If you know a child who likes toys and admires superheroes, firefighters, sports stars or princesses, along with a plethora of other themes, chances are they already have a "collection" of action figures.

Or perhaps you have a box of action figures saved from your childhood or from your children that you now can pass on to another kiddo in your life. With a little guidance and encouragement, owning toys can take on a new meaning.

Transforming a group of action figures into a collection doesn't mean taking all the fun out of the toys, however. Figures purchased as playthings should continue to be enjoyed. But grouping action figures selected for a true collection together by theme,

Bernard and Jose Flores with a table of action figures at a collectibles show.

cleverly displaying them and learning to value and care for them are some of the lessons that adult collectors can easily share with a child. And, of course, there's the joy of procuring new figures for a growing collection. It's always fun to get a new toy.

Once you get the existing toys in a budding collection categorized, you can think about ways to add more. Fortunately, single action figures stocked on the shelves of toy stores and large retailers usually can be purchased for less than $25 new in the package. Playmobil and LEGO also offer sets including action figures at many price points, including those in the $5-$10 range. Children can save their allowance for these purchases, which also are great additions to birthday and holiday wish lists.

Bobbi Boyd, co-founder of Raving Toy Maniac, suggests the offerings of fast food restaurants as a place to start, too. "Fast food restaurants tend to have toys in their kids' meals, and depending on the license, the toy could be an action figure. Many times the restaurant will have a 'girl toy' promotion running at the same time as the 'boy toy' promotion, so you

This 1977 action figure of R2–D2 is on a blister card and is in mint condition, making it an excellent find for would–be toy collectors.

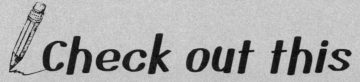

Check out this

entertaining online destination for action figure collectors...

**Toy and Action Figure Museum –
ActionFigureMuseum.com**

With fun activities like group tours, along with special action figure and toy exhibits, collectors of all ages can appreciate the Action Figure Museum located in Pauls Valley, Oklahoma. If you can't make it to Oklahoma to see it in person, visit online for what amounts to an amazing tour.

might see Barbie-themed toys at the same time as Spider-Man toys at the same restaurant. Some restaurants will sell the toy separately, so you aren't stuck buying the meal if it's not the kind of food you want to feed your child."

Boyd also considers thrift stores to be a fantastic resource for finding action figures on a limited budget. "Depending on the store and how they display their merchandise, action figures could be jumbled up in a big bin you could have fun digging through and exploring, or they could be bagged up with a few similar figures," Boyd said. "Be sure to keep an eye out for play sets and vehicles, too – anything that could be a new 'playground' for the action figures you already have. If Spider-Man can fit into the A-Team van, he can drive it.

"I don't think anything you would find toy-wise in a thrift store would be especially valuable, but I do believe

that searching for the toys and figures in thrift stores could be a fun activity for parents and children to do together," Boyd said. "You just never know what will turn up on a trip there, and the 'toy budget' lasts longer in a thrift store."

The same shopping strategies can apply to garage sales and flea markets. Look for items completing sets and themes that already interest your collecting buddy as well as those adding new categories of action figures to expand a collection.

And don't forget those action figures you might already have packed away. That's how Eric Bradley, of Texas, helped his son, Patrick, get started as an action figure collector.

"Lucky for him, my mother was a collector and never got rid of the toys I had when I was a kid," Bradley said. "I loved action figures growing up and

This collection of 1970s carded action figures, and boxed Joker Mobile, sold for more than $1,500.

had lots from the '70s and '80s. Pat started playing with them when he was young, and the interest grew from there."

Patrick Bradley

Patrick, who started collecting when he was just 5, enjoyed having mini versions of his favorite characters from comic books and movies to play with and display, along with studying all their minute details. What fun for Bradley, too, as they played together with things he remembered fondly!

Learning to categorize and store collectibles safely is a great learning opportunity for kids through most any type of collection, and action figures are no exception. Bradley, who helps his son shop for action figures at flea markets, department stores, and comic book shows, suggests using boxes individually spaced with separators to store figures still in great condition. Those well-loved figures that have seen a lot of action already can be grouped together in a larger box until it's time to play again.

Deciding exactly what children want their action figures to be doing on any given day is all part of the excitement. There are many tutorials online for making action figure displays using photographs and other props, and kids can learn to use their imagination as well.

Bradley said his son really enjoyed making up elaborate sets and headquarters out of cardboard boxes when he was younger, and he learned how to become a better artist in the process. Patrick studied the details, molding, and accessories and used those in intricate drawings. The figures served as models for his art.

But as Bradley also noted, enjoying action figures in creative display settings requires taking them out of the packages. As a veteran collector and author of a number of antiques and collectibles guidebooks, he suggests carefully removing the toys and keeping the packages, just in

Free from his box, this action figure can roam the world of a child's imagination.

case those particular figures turn out to be something pricey down the road. Having the original packaging always adds to the value of a collectible.

Value, however, is a tricky topic when it comes to collecting action figures. "Not to sound like the Grinch, but I think the most important thing in this case is that collecting action figures should be a fun thing that parents and kids can do together," Boyd said. "If they take the approach that this is something to do as an investment, maybe they should stick to stocks or other traditional investments."

Nevertheless, some action figures are quite valuable, so don't rule out running across one of them on a shopping foray. Most often, such finds are older action figures. Not as many were produced when they were new, and people didn't think they might be valuable some day, so they didn't save them in the original box. The lack of supply to meet current demand from adult collectors makes those figures worth more.

For example, consider Star Wars figures from the 1970s. If you have some of those, or run across them, before playing with them, do a Google search or look them up on eBay.com to see what similar items are selling for. Newer Star Wars figures produced in the past 20 years or so are less likely rare and valuable because too many of them were saved new-in-package specifically as collectibles.

Boyd offered this advice to collectors of new action figures: "If you still have an eye on the future value, either do not open the packaging or buy one to open and one to keep sealed, and be sure to keep all of the packaging and accessories. Keep the figures clean and in good condition."

Most action figures worth a good sum are purchased and traded by adult collectors rather than kids. But the child you're nurturing now as a collector probably will grow up appreciating the lessons you taught about retaining value, not only as it applies to action figures but to any future collecting endeavors.

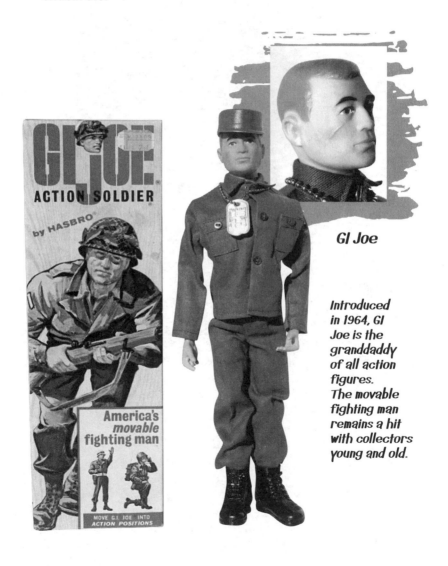

GI Joe

Introduced in 1964, GI Joe is the granddaddy of all action figures. The movable fighting man remains a hit with collectors young and old.

A rare prototype resign cast of Michaelangelo from Teenage Mutant Ninja Turtle fame, 1987.

One of the most prized action figures of the Star Wars universe, bounty hunter Boba Fett

Arguably the greatest
Bad Guy ever introduced
in the movies, Darth
Vader is equally popular
among action figure fans.

There are few
toys created in the
50-year history
of action figures
that evoke such
fond memories
as Kenner's Luke
Skywalker.

"Collecting for the sheer joy of possessing the signature of someone whom a child ardently admires should be the main objective in pursuing these collectibles."

AUTOGRAPHS – GARNERING A SIGNATURE COLLECTION

What should you look for when exploring collecting hobbies for children? Ranking high on most lists: affordability, relative ease, learning and, perhaps most of all, fun. Autograph collecting encompasses all these attributes into one neat hobby, and it's something kids can grow with over time, easily carrying their newfound passion for collecting into adulthood.

If you're not an autograph collector yourself but think this sounds intriguing for a child in your life, don't let fear of the unknown keep you from getting a collection underway. Both experts and seasoned collectors – many of whom have collected autographs since they were kids – can guide you.

Autograph collecting usually transpires in one of three ways: asking for a signature in person, requesting one by mail, or by purchasing through a memorabilia dealer either at a show or via the Internet. While purchasing autographs might seem the easiest route to putting together a nice collection, it's not the method that experienced autograph collectors usually

Autograph of Jim Davis, artist of the "Garfield" cartoon.
Courtesy of Heritage Auctions, ha.com

recommend. Dale Nehring, of Illinois, who started collecting autographs when he was 9 and now has close to 300,000 examples, advises an alternative for his own grandchildren.

"Beware of buying autographs online," Nehring said. "There are many unscrupulous dealers who blatantly sell forgeries. Never just assume that because it's advertised to have a certificate of authenticity that it's authentic. Certificates are only as good as the person who wrote them." If an autograph is issued a certificate of authenticity (COA) by a reputable service, such as PSA/DNA Authentication Services or James Spence, there is a good chance it's the real deal. Such authentication comes with a price, however, that might make an autograph unaffordable for the average child.

Autographs expert John Hickey suggests taking a shot at obtaining signatures in person when beginning a collection with children. "The personal approach, while not always successful, is obviously the only real way to be sure the signature is authentic," Hickey said.

Most experts agree that adults can help kids get started by taking them to a low-key event, like off-season training sessions for sports teams or small-venue shows for other celebrities, to avoid throngs of autograph seekers that might overwhelm youngsters. Taking a photograph or sports card along to be autographed is quite acceptable, but index cards also work as a low-cost alternative.

If in-person collecting is not an option, both Nehring and Hickey acknowledge that collecting autographs by mail – referred to by collectors as "Through The Mail" (TTM) – is a viable alternative when approached with some guidance.

To collect autographs by mail, some basic supplies are required: paper, envelopes, stamps, and address lists. TTM collectors sometimes send an item along with their request, such as a photo or piece of memorabilia relating to the celebrity. Again, index cards work as well. A self-addressed stamped envelope (SASE) should also be included so the signed item can easily be returned. It's also wise to realize that making a mail request will not always net a signature, so there will likely be some initial expense on supplies and stamps with no return on that investment.

"Not every request is guaranteed to get an autograph," offered longtime collector David Kahan, of Massachusetts. "The best thing to do is to send the autograph request and then forget about it. When you get something back, it is a reward. Many of us send out hundreds of requests and if we get a 50 percent success rate, we're happy."

Children can learn discipline, organization, and patience through collecting autographs, noted Richard Kim, of

OLYMPIA 1911

WALT DISNEY PRODUCTIONS
MICKEY MOUSE
SOUND CARTOONS
2719 HYPERION
HOLLYWOOD

October 18, 1934.

Miss Rose T. Marucci,
109 Lloyd Street,
New Haven, Connecticut.

My dear Miss Marucci:

It has been our experience in developing young artists for our highly specialized type of work that the teaching of art in many of the academies throughout the country greatly over-emphasizes the study and appreciation of art, but minimizes the stress that should be put on the development of fundamentals and draftsmanship. It is our theory that artistic ability develops naturally while the execution and technique of the arts comes only after much hard work and practice.

A person may be a great artist, capable of great visualism, but he may be unable to execute his thoughts and ideas because of his lack of knowledge of draftsmanship and application. A thorough study of life and nature is essential to the development of talent. Every artist should be able to thoroughly analyze emotions, sensations and reactions. In my estimation, the same requirements apply to any line of art, whether it be drawing, painting, carica-tures, music, photography or even cooking!

When a person has thoroughly and definitely acquired the fundamen-tals of drawing (which in our business is good draftsmanship) and has added to this fundamental knowledge, visualism and creativeness, he is then known as a true artist -- and sometimes he is called a genius.

Please understand that my views, as expressed above, are made en-tirely with respect to our type of work - the art of cartoon ani-mation.

Thank you for writing me and I hope this brief note may be of some help to you and the other students in your research work.

Sincerely yours,

Walt Disney

WD:DV

SILLY SYMPHONY
Sound Cartoons

**Walt Disney signed letter
on company letterhead,
1934, 11" x 8-1/2".**
Courtesy of Heritage Auctions, ha.com

Jacksons Victory Tour program, signed "Michael Jackson" on cover in black pen, 14" x 11".
Courtesy of Julien's Auctions, www.juliensauctions.com

Arizona, a lifelong autograph enthusiast and developer of MemReg.com, an online resource where memorabilia and autographs can be cataloged to document provenance and preserve value. In addition, Kim said, young collectors can learn even more about the people who entertain them as well as what makes them autograph-worthy.

"Depending on the kind of collection, as the child relearns more about the person, he or she will also learn more about the subject matter, so it can be quite educational," Kim said. He also sees autograph collecting as something parents and kids can do together when looking for ways to balance the amount of time spent on the purely electronic world of gaming and texting.

"If your child is into games or comics, then you can start by writing to the game creator to get an autograph to put the 'human' factor back into the games," Kim said. Such advice applies to any pop culture figure the child in your life may admire, and most experts agree that keeping the focus narrow in the beginning makes autograph collecting more

Michael Jordan hand-signed NBA Chicago Bulls basketball jersey.
Courtesy of J. Sugarman Auction Corp., www.jaysugarman.com

manageable for kids.

Looking at the hobby in this light takes it beyond movie stars, sports figures and popular musicians, urging children to explore other interests they may have. Take history, for example. Autographs of historical significance often interest youngsters with a penchant for the past.

Owning an autograph related to a person of historical significance who intrigues or inspires a child can be the next best thing to actually meeting that figure. "It's an intimate thing. After all, this is a person's handwriting we're speaking of," said Sandra Palomino, who specializes in historical manuscripts in her work for Heritage Auctions.

"I work with clients who share that they started at age 10 and younger with an interest in a particular historical figure, and they're still collectors into their 60s and 70s," Palomino said. Many times a parent, grandparent or mentor will gift to a child an item related to a historical event or

Sandra Palomino

person they somehow have been involved with, and that piques curiosity.

Palomino noted that presidential autographs can be readily found, and some "clipped" signatures are very affordable. A clipped signature in the autograph world is one obtained from a document or letter. These can sell for as little as $20-$30, depending on the particular president.

Parents guiding children in collecting clipped signatures should encourage them to look for authentic signatures written in ink on personal correspondence or official documents. And keep in mind that most mass-produced congratulatory letters from the White House are autopen signatures applied by an assistant. While these items might be interesting to own if they were sent to a family member, they don't have the weight or value when compared to a signature penned by a president's own hand.

Also, realize that there's no guarantee that autographs are going to appreciate in value over time. In fact, when pop stars and sports figures slip into obscurity in the decades following their heyday, their autographs may even lose value. Collecting for the sheer joy of possessing the signature of someone whom a child ardently admires should be the main objective in pursuing these collectibles.

Sandra Palomino specializes in historical manuscripts in her work for Heritage Auctions.

There are, however, instances when a rookie player or budding musician will move on to become a legend, and an early autograph may turn out to be rare and worth a pretty penny. With this in mind, as well as preserving memories related to obtaining this type of memorabilia in the first place, autographs should be stored safely.

"As with most collectibles, you need to store them in a dry, cool location. For autographs, avoiding direct sunlight is the key

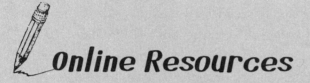

Online Resources

There are many online resources for growing an autograph collection. Here are several expert-recommended websites that can supply addresses for Through The Mail collecting:

MemReg.com – Free site offering an extensive database of addresses and more information on registering and collecting autographs and related memorabilia.

Fanmail.biz – This site also offers a TTM address database free of charge.

SportsCollectors.net – For a small fee, this resource provides a wealth of information for collectors specializing in sports autographs.

SportsAddressLists.com – If you're willing to invest a bit more for sports-related signatures, this site sells a comprehensive list of addresses and more reasonably priced specialized lists available as well.

to keeping them from fading, and do not alter them in any way," Kim advised. Altering includes writing or placing stickers on them, folding them and puncturing them. Autographs can be displayed by framing them using acid-free materials. They can also be stored safely in binders filled with non-acidic storage sleeves.

With proper direction, and perhaps a small financial boost to get them started, children can indeed amass, enjoy, and preserve a collection of autographs that reflect a lifetime of learning and enjoyment.

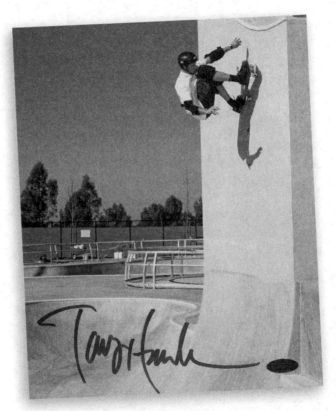

Tony Hawk autographed 8" x 10" photograph.
Courtesy of Heritage Auctions, ha.com

Allowing lists to guide a collection helps to narrow possibilities that at first may seem overwhelming."

— James Gannon

Chapter 7

BOOKS – INTRODUCING THE WONDER-FILLED WORLD OF THE BIBLIOPHILE

At a point when leisurely reading often means picking up an electronic device, would a young person ever consider collecting "dead tree" books? It might not be the easiest sell, considering kids these days are coming of age when mainstream brick-and-mortar bookstores are becoming more of a rarity. But the increasing novelty, similar to that with record albums and stereo turntables, actually points to this genre of collectibles becoming

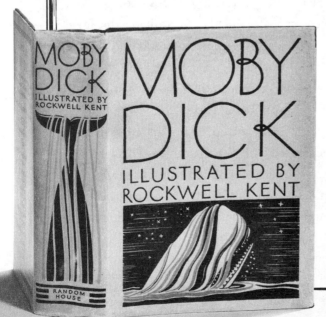

Herman Melville's Moby Dick was written in 1851, yet it remains today a timeless work of fiction for readers and collectors alike.

more attractive as young people discover the nostalgia associated with book collecting.

So where does nurturing the young bibliophile begin? Susan Benne, executive director of the Antiquarian Booksellers' Association of America, suggests reading with children as a first step. Allow them to fall in love with books by making up stories to go with the pictures, even if they're too young to grasp the words. As they get older, noticing an emerging interest and sharing a few volumes with a budding book enthusiast can spark an interest in collecting.

Ryan Julian, who won the National Collegiate Book Collecting Contest in 2010, picked up his first book on the history of mathematics as a teen while working on a research paper. This one book changed Julian's view of mathematics forever by giving him insight into how modern disciplines were first formulated, and his newfound appreciation led him to seek out another book on the topic. A teacher who had mentored Julian's interest in math for many years gave him several more historical mathematics-related books to spur him on. That simple act of sharing led to an expanded collection Julian continued to build and share with others. In fact, his book collection not only earned accolades but also warranted a display at the University of Chicago's Joseph Regenstein Library.

"In addition to my main collection on the history of mathematics, I also have a smaller collection of books relating to the history of science and a number of early American textbooks," Julian said. "I think it's extremely important to first find a subject area or theme that truly fascinates you. This will not only help you to identify and understand the nuances of the individual items in your collection, but it will also ensure that your interest will sustain the development of the collection for years to come."

Famously made into a radio drama by Orson Welles in 1938, The War of The Worlds by H.G. Wells remains a science fiction classic.

James Gannon, who oversees rare books for Heritage Auctions, also emphasizes focus when helping a young person start a book collection. For instance, a youngster interested in collecting children's literature or picture books can set out to duplicate the winners appearing on past Newbery or Caldecott Medal lists. Allowing lists to guide a collection helps to narrow possibilities that at first may seem overwhelming.

Gannon also suggests visiting used bookstores where, with some patience and diligence, you can find older editions of books at affordable prices. These probably won't end up being extremely valuable first editions or even moderately valued second editions. But he cites older books as generally more interesting and often of higher quality in terms of binding and materials when compared to recent reprints.

Teaching children about the value of first-edition books can also be a rewarding lesson. If you have an opportunity to shop garage sales, estate sales, and thrift stores where used books are frequently sold, look together for those elusive treasures. While you may never actually run across a first edition in one of those settings, it never hurts to know the potential value of such collectibles.

Even first editions of children's picture books can be worth quite a good sum. According to 1stEdition.net, there are more than 40 picture books with a value of $1,000 or more. *Where The Wild Things Are* by Maurice Sendak, first published in 1963, tops the list with a value of $6,200 in very good condition. The price

Theo and Yenna Lee–Gannon visit with a favorite author, Cornelia Maria Funke, a German author of children's fiction. Funke took the time to carefully inscribe and even illustration copies Theo and Yenna brought to a book signing event. "You can see she included great drawings and took a lot of time with them," said father James Gannon, Director of Fine Books at Heritage Auctions. "They took her thank you cards with drawings based on her characters."

91

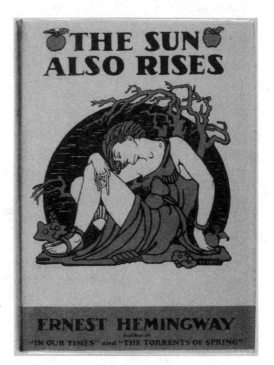

First published in 1926, Hemingway's masterpiece is the quintessential novel of the Lost Generation. As such it is adored by collectors.

swells to more than $10,000 in excellent condition. Many other first editions published within the past 15-25 years, including *Shrek!* by William Steig, first printed in 1990, might sell to an avid collector in the $80-$160 range, depending on the condition of the book.

When asked about identifying first editions, Gannon shared that each publisher marks first editions differently. He suggests visiting websites like AbeBooks.com and AlephBet.com to start researching used books in a child's collection, to determine which edition they have and what it might be worth. AbeBooks also features a video on identifying first editions as part of its Basic Guide to Book Collecting. 1stEdition.net offers some great tutorials to help collectors learn about first editions as well.

Edgar Rice Burroughs' novel premiered in 1912 and was so popular that he wrote two dozen sequels.

Don't overlook second-edition books. "Second-edition books are often essentially the same book as first editions, perhaps with very minor changes or none at all," said Gannon, who once built an entire collection based solely on second editions. They won't be as highly valued as first editions but hold more worth than later runs of the same book and merit noting in a collection. Second editions can be researched in the same manner as first editions using information gleaned from the book's title page.

For older children and teens showing an interest in books, online is a good place to start exploring for books at affordable prices and researching them. Actually visiting an antiquarian bookstore to pique a youngster's interest, however, could open up a new world filled with books ripe for discovery.

Web Resources for Book Collecting

From book collecting basics every collector should review to identifying first editions, these resources are recommended by book collecting pros:

The AbeBooks Book Collecting Guide – Find the link under the "Rare Books" tab at AbeBooks.com

Basics on Valuing Books and Identifying First Editions – Click on "Collector Information" at BMDBooks.com

Antiquarian Booksellers' Association of America Book Fairs – Click on "Events" at ABAA.org

National Collegiate Book Collecting Contest – Click on "About the ABAA" at ABAA.org

Ian Kahn, proprietor of Lux Mentis Booksellers, in Portland, Maine, has collected books since he was a child growing up among avid readers in what he describes as a "house of books." Now, he guides his son, Aidan, who collects and deals in miniature books, and thoroughly enjoys entertaining young collectors in his store. "I love having kids and young people show an interest and will go on about various elements for as long as they can stand it," Kahn said. "The key is to find out what they are interested in and letting that define the direction."

When visiting an antiquarian bookstore, ask the shopkeeper to point you in the direction of books based on the interest of the child. Take note of what the children define as "cool" as you browse the stacks together. Even though they may not be able to afford particular books now, time spent in such a setting can provide some insight on how to direct them as you approach building a collection suitable to the child's interests and budget.

Children also need to learn proper book handing to keep their collections in good condition and maintain value. Asking an antiquarian book dealer for hands-on guidance in this area could be a fruitful part of a trip to the bookstore.

Books won't be the right collecting choice for every young person, since a certain maturity level comes into play here, and book collectors often have a penchant for reading that not every child will possess. But with some guidance, a kid exhibiting an interest can build a collection that entertains, educates and carries them into adulthood surrounded by the wonder-filled world of the bibliophile.

Narrowing the Focus: More on Collecting Children's Books

Once upon a time, a little girl fell in love with books and inspired her parents to start a collection. While certainly no fairy tale, in a number of ways this story is a dream come true for husband and wife Noah Fleisher and Lauren Zittle, along with their 10-year-old daughter, Fiona.

Published in 1952, Charlotte's Web, written by E.B. White and illustrated by Garth Williams, is equally a joy to read and to collect.

More than 38 million copies of The Very Hungry Caterpillar have been sold, but first editions with the dust jacket are in high demand.

In late 2015, Fleisher and Zittle published *Collecting Children's Books: Art, Memories, Values* to share their passion on the topic with others. While Fleisher had daily exposure to some of the finest collectibles in the world as former public relations director for Heritage Auctions, Zittle wasn't really much of a collector until Fiona came along and motivated her mother to dive head first into a pool swimming with colorful characters – children's literature.

"I was a bookworm and I really looked forward to sharing all those books I'd loved with my daughter," Zittle said. As a mom, she also knows that reading at an early age includes benefits such as exercising the brain, doing better in school, and improving concentration. As time passed, she noticed even broader rewards from reading, such as developing empathy and a connection with the human experience.

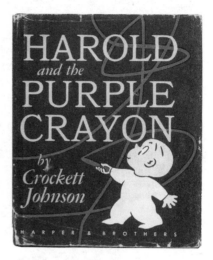

A Caldecott nominee published in 1998, No, David, *is a great book for any beginning collector.*

Harold and the Purple Crayon *won the 1956 Caldecott Medal. A first edition is worth about $1,000.*

"Our scolding usually consists of telling her to stop reading so she can set the table," Zittle shared. Fiona is not only a great kid and a remarkable student, but she also shows an interest in the world around her gleaned through reading about fascinating themes and interesting places she wouldn't know otherwise.

Beyond introducing her daughter to children's books – with the help of Fleisher, of course – Zittle gets what it means to be a collector now. Through this journey, she learned about the labor of love found in compiling a collection and how it offers a keen connection to the past. Sharing a decade-by-decade overview of favorites and a number of authors who stand out as the best of the best in *Collecting Children's Books* reflects this newfound appreciation.

As an ardent collectibles enthusiast, Fleisher believes amassing a collection of children's books should be about buying what you love. As a collection grows, he advises narrowing the focus by looking at a certain author, theme, or time period, and the captivating book he wrote with his wife helps collectors do just that. This is true for collectors of all ages, even kids who might show an interest in really building a collection of books they're drawn to.

A way to do that is visiting book and paper shows or bookshops specializing in collectibles as a family. "I tend to default to people in the business when it comes to learning and

Book Care 101
with James Gannon, Director of Fine Books at Heritage Auctions.

James Gannon, one of Heritage Auctions' rare book experts, suggests reminding kids of these book care basics:

- Remove books from the shelf correctly by pushing in the volumes to either side and grasping the book at the center rather than the top of the spine, where it can tear.

- Take care not to extend a book too far when opening it, to protect the binding.

- Always use a bookmark to hold your place rather than laying a book flat with the pages open.

- Never eat or drink while handling a book you want to preserve, especially collectible books.

James Gannon

guidance, so book dealers are a good resource," Fleisher said. "Many auction houses have book specialists on staff as well. And the Heritage archives online are a great place for research and looking through high-quality photos."

Beyond all that Heritage offers at HA.com, *Collecting Children's Books* recommends a number of collector resources found online. Again, sites like AbeBooks.com and Alibris.com are recommended, along with other reputable book dealers and auctioneers who sell books. Such resources can be tapped for research as well as shopping.

When buying children's literature, whether guiding a young collector or for your own bookshelf, Fleisher and Zittle recommend paying close attention to the condition of covers, which should be clean and not faded. Spines should be in good shape, too, not broken or cracked. And if the book is supposed to have a dust jacket, make sure it is present, clean and original. Teach children to check pages for foxing (age-related spots or browning) and water damage, along with any that are torn or missing. Such factors greatly impact the value of any type of book.

Fleisher and Zittle also encourage buyers to do pricing research before shopping to know what similar copies have sold for. When

Chris Van Allsburg's out-of-control classic about a decidedly evil board game was published in 1981.

Curious George, by H.A. and Margaret Rey, is a perennial classic dating back to 1941.

The Poky Little Puppy is one of the first 12 Little Golden Books published in 1942.

considering a signed or inscribed edition, make every effort to ensure that the signature is authentic before paying a premium for that perk.

"If you are not buying it in person, then ask these questions in advance. It will show you know what you are doing and make sure you are getting the best book for your money," the authors share in their book. Shop online together with the kids you're mentoring so they can learn these valuable lessons while building a collection, too.

Whether buying online or in person, don't forget to look for edition and printing information within children's volumes, just as you would with any other type of literature. The first printing of a first edition can be far more valuable than other copies that might look the same at first glance. "The edition information is always on the copyright page, listed toward the bottom," noted Fleisher and Zittle. Ask online sellers to forward

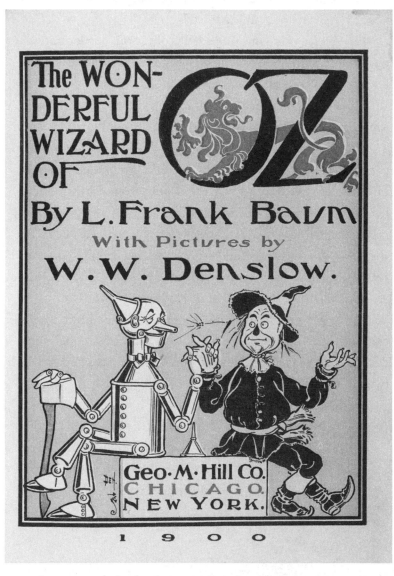

There are few books that can claim the cultural influence of L. Frank Baum's The Wonderful Wizard of Oz, 1900.

a photo of the page to you so you can help a youngster decipher the information, if needed. This all goes back to knowing what you're buying before pulling the trigger.

Of course, after amassing a true collection, one looming question remains: Should you actually sit down and read those books with a youngster?

"It depends on the level of collecting and how much you spend on the books," Fleisher said. "The Oz books, for instance. There are lots of editions to choose from, and there are some good reading copies available out there." If you spend thousands on a first edition, in other words, it would obviously be better left for occasional admiration rather than risk damaging it with repeated reading. There are, however, many books available in the $20-$50 range that could serve both as collection books and readers, when handled with care.

Fiona has her own shelf of books that count as her collection rather than reading copies. That's in addition to the examples Zittle more purposely sought out as her collecting curiosity grew. Other books the family owns have been read over and over again.

With some research, care, and lots of fun together

discovering the delight of children's books, this family is living happily ever after. Through the magic of collecting, maybe yours can, too.

Collecting Children's Books co-authors Noah Fleisher and Lauren Zittle with their daughter, Fiona.

Chapter 8

COINS AND BANK NOTES – NURTURING THE NUMISMATIST

Ask a dozen successful coin experts when they first began collecting and you can bet the majority started young. No, they didn't imagine their childhood love of sifting through pocket change and studying the intricacies of their discoveries would actually amount to a career one day. But thousands of

Proof 1974–S Kennedy half dollar.

"The more coins you get to look at and examine, the more opportunities you have to learn."
— Miles Standish

coins and decades later, they're still immersed in the world of numismatics.

As a prime example, take Miles Standish, a coin industry innovator and grading pro. Standish started collecting when he was just 9 and really got a boost when his father began encouraging his love for coins. "My dad really supported my interest and shared my enthusiasm. We learned together," Standish said.

As a teenager, Standish began to master the ins and outs of coin grading. One of his specialties back then was silver dollars. He sold his first one for a profit when he was 13. He traveled to trade shows, continued to expand his knowledge, and by the age of 19, he took a job with the American Numismatic Association (ANA). He currently serves as vice president for the Numismatic Guaranty Corp. Standish still loves those silver dollars, too. As the author of *American Silver Eagles: A Guide to the U.S. Bullion Coin Program* and *Morgan Dollar: America's Love Affair with a Legendary Coin* (both Whitman Publishing), he shares this affinity with others.

"I developed an eye for it as I learned how to properly examine and handle coins at a young age," said Standish, proving you can never start too early when nurturing collectors, and you just never know where a hobby will lead.

Chris Bierrenbach, Executive Vice President of International Numismatics for Heritage Auctions, also started amassing a coin collection early – at age 8. His grandmother bought him a catalog to help identify some old coins passed down from his great-grandfather. Bierrenbach's passion for the hobby grew exponentially.

By the time he was in his 20s, Bierrenbach's interest in coins led him to a rewarding profession. After obtaining a degree in

management, he founded Bier Numismatica, which grew to be one of the largest collectible coin purveyors in Latin America. At 30, he became the youngest-ever technical director for the Brazilian Numismatic Society, and he founded the Latin American Numismatic Convention, setting a great example for young collectors following his lead.

When offering advice on getting kids interested in coins today, Bierrenbach suggests introducing them to the hobby through means accessible to everyone. His ideas include completing a set of all 50 state quarters or filling coin folders with Lincoln cents (known as pennies to most kids). If a neophyte collector starts showing significant interest, he said, "Engage them in the hobby by encouraging them to join local clubs, attend seminars, visit coin shows and auctions together or doing a coin exhibition."

Standish recommends that enthusiastic young collectors get as much hands-on experience with numismatics as they can as early as possible. He agrees that visiting coin shows and shops offer a great way to handle coins that have already been graded, since learning about the basics in that area will always be important to collectors. Coin auction previews, like those held by Heritage Auctions, are another way to examine a variety of examples without spending – or buying – even a dime. That is, unless you want to partake in the excitement of bidding as you show a young collector the ropes.

"The more coins you get to look at and examine, the more opportunities you have to learn," Standish said. In-person visits also allow kids to pose questions to experienced dealers and collectors. Adults in the business realize the importance of encouraging budding enthusiasts, and many are very forthcoming and helpful as mentors when it comes to nurturing

*State quarters for
Wisconsin and California.*

Professional grading services can take the guesswork out of coin collecting, especially when buying.

interest. Some even continue building relationships through email with older kids and teens, so it never hurts to ask the friendly folks you meet for their business cards.

Standish encourages kids to read everything they can find about their favorite types of coins, studying prices realized online through Heritage's website at HA.com, and utilizing both online and app-based resources for smartphones to learn more about grading and values. Professional Coin Grading Service (PCGS) even offers a spiffy phone-based app to help with grading that allows you to place your examples right next to high-resolution photos of United States coins of all ages and denominations.

For further study, Bierrenbach also suggests buying an interested child a copy of the *Red Book*, also known as *A Guide Book of United States Coins,* by Kenneth Bressett and

R.S. Yoeman (Whitman Publishing), for further study. For kids expressing interest in world varieties, he recommends the *Standard Catalog of World Coins* by George S. Cuhaj and Thomas Michael (Krause Publications). Both of these books are updated yearly, and ardent coin hunters always have the latest editions close at hand. "They're the most popular and a good place to start," Bierrenbach said.

Another fantastic resource both Bierrenbach and Standish agree upon is the Young Numismatist program sponsored by ANA. A visit to money.org will inform both adults and kids on many worthwhile programs that are both educational and fun for a small yearly fee. Young Numismatist resources include scholarships and summer seminars for teens. The summer seminars can prove to be particularly valuable since they cover important topics such as honing grading skills and identifying fakes.

Of course, just as with other collecting genres, you can't force an interest in coins. What you can do is present the idea and provide a few basic resources for getting started. If the child under your wing really seems enthused once they get rolling, help them take the hobby a step forward and see where the journey leads. Imagine how exciting it would be to nurture an up-and-coming expert who could soon be teaching you a thing or two about coins.

Ancient Coins to Earn While They Learn

Keeping children engaged and excited about collecting as they approach their teen years isn't always easy for parents and educators. But for kids with even a slight interest in coin collecting, the lure of "free money" offered through the American Numismatic Association's (ANA) Ancient Coin Project provides young teens a way to earn while they learn.

Ancient world coins, like this Roman Denarious, are incredibly interesting, providing both a history and numismatic lesson.

The ANA David R. Cervin Ancient Coin Project, named in honor of its founder, began several decades ago, serving young collectors with an interest in earning an array of ancient coins. By writing articles or reports, making presentations in school or to Boy or Girl Scout troops, and completing other projects the kids find interesting, participants earn coins as a reward for their efforts.

ANA's Young Numismatist (YN) program offers a number of options for parents or mentors exploring options to get, or keep, young people interested in learning about a variety of coins, including ancient examples. "The ANA realizes that the future of our hobby is in the hands of the youngsters of today. It is in the best interest of the ANA and of the hobby in general to get as many youngsters involved in numismatics as possible," said ANA Education Director Rod Gillis.

But for the kids participating, earning some exceptionally cool coins while achieving step-by-step goals keeps them both interested and entertained. Matt Tormey, a Massachusetts native, started the project when he was 13. Two of the coins he earned – an Antoninianus (double denarius) from the Gallo-Roman Empire, A.D. 268-270, and a Roman Empire silver denarius issued during the rule of Septimius Severus, A.D. 193-211 – provided some interesting stories when he researched them.

"My favorite is the silver denarius," Tormey said. He found the coin to be fascinating because it shows a Roman sitting on a shield with a scepter in one hand while the other grasps a Palladium (a statue of a female figure found in Roman mythology). The head on the obverse is Septimius himself. "It's silver, a precious metal, which is also very cool, and it's just a perfect example of Roman mintage at its height."

Cole Schenewerk, from California, a former Young Numismatist of the Year, entered the project when he was just 9. He earned all eight coins and the book offered through the program. The silver denarius is also his favorite.

"It isn't the most expensive coin, but the history behind the family dynamics of the dynasty makes for some interesting reading," Schenewerk said. "Septimius Severus's son, Caracalla, ordered the murder of his brother, as well as his ex-wife and her whole immediate family. Historian Edward Gibbon called him 'the common enemy of mankind.' Not a person I'd like to know personally."

In "A Story of Two Coins," a two-part feature published by *The California Numismatist,* Schenewerk shared his research about the first two coins he earned. This effort yielded another

The Roman Emperor Balbinus is shown on this double denarious, AD 238. The two clasped hands signify unity.

ancient coin for his collection, and in his own words, he "truly enjoyed" the experience.

Learning more about these coins clearly proves to be part of the fun of earning them, but the tasks completed to garner them don't always involve examples featured in the project.

"I got the first coin talking in school about a set of three ancient Chinese coins from the Han dynasty," Tormey said. "While researching these coins, I found that only the ancient Chinese put a square hole in the coin. Also, the ancient Chinese coins had holes to be strung together for safekeeping. Learning about and explaining theses coins to my fellow schoolmates and teachers was a fun way to share my hobby with others."

From the perspective of an educator, Gillis believes the most noteworthy message children learn from the project is that hard work and diligence will result in significant rewards. "Another important lesson learned is that patience is a key attribute in seeing any project through," Gillis said. "We like to believe that the lessons learned from the Ancient Coin Project will not only help youngsters as numismatists but serve as lessons used throughout their lives."

Harlan J. Berk, owner of a coin business in Chicago and one of the hobby's most respected experts on ancient coins, has provided many examples distributed through the project. He believes the young people participating in the program, who obviously possess both driven personalities and a passion for collecting, relish "winning the prize" and the thrill of competition. "The value of earning the top award is doing just that, reaching a difficult goal," Berk said.

Of course, nurturing a hobby that can enrich the lives of kids for years to come is the reason the Ancient Coin Project exists, and why Berk has donated coins for the program. He knows the project can be the first step in a lifelong journey brimming with rewards. He wants to share that intangible gift even more than the intrinsic coins he has provided. "My motivation is the old and trite 'why not give back?'" Berk said.

Participants in the program, while young, also look to the future. "I would hope that my kids are interested in coin collecting, and if they are, I would encourage them to participate in the Ancient Coin Project," Schenewerk said. "The coins are very valuable and tell interesting stories of times long past. I hope to encourage lots of kids to participate in this program."

Tormey agrees. "When I get older, I would love for my

kids to do this project," Tormey said. "It is a fun, educational and rewarding way to share and savor our favorite hobby: coin collecting."

World Bank Notes: A Collection Worth More Than Face Value

Think about what you would like to see in a collection to share with loved ones. Chances are, long-term growth in value would be high on the list. But what if you could find a collection to share with your kids or grandkids that goes way beyond the face value of each object right now? Reaching far beyond the intrinsic, world bank notes may be the perfect, most timeless collectible you can find for kids.

Dustin Johnston, director of currency auctions for Heritage Auctions, knows firsthand how amusing and educational world bank note collecting can be. He got his start when he was about 9, and it's a journey he's still pursuing. He has his grandpa to thank for that.

"My grandfather first split his collection between my sister and me, which began my interest in numismatics," Johnston recalled. "The grouping was heavily world coins and paper money from Europe where he served in World War II."

Thoroughly intrigued, this budding enthusiast went to the library and checked out books to learn more about all the colorful bank notes in the collection. One of the first things he wanted to find out was who got the better end of the deal, he or his sister. Even though he discovered that his sister's share was worth a bit more money than his, he continued to explore the culture and artistry held in his newfound interest in currency.

"The designs are incredibly beautiful," Johnston said. "They include agriculture, industry, wildlife and many others. It's fun to find different examples from each country that fit these

Excellent examples of five bank notes from the Reserve Bank of Austrailia.

Foreign paper money is not only beautiful to collect but it broadens children's world perspective.

themes. Animals are popular with kids, too. It's a great way to put together a menagerie."

But a collection like this doesn't have to stop at something fun for a child to do in their spare time. These affordable little works of art can actually take some of the drudgery out of school projects to make learning both entertaining and cool. World currency makes an enviable show-and-tell grouping to share with classmates, and the individual notes can be woven into projects and reports on an array of subjects.

"One thing that really helped me was using my collection as a foundation for what we were learning in school. I tried to incorporate it into every class," Johnston said. The detailed engravings of people and places on the notes lent to varied history lessons. Mapping where the currency originated helped with locating countries around the globe for geography class. And what the money was made of and how it is formed provided the basis for a clever chemistry project.

Johnston also finds that world bank notes provide an economical pursuit as a hobby and an ideal introduction to collecting. Kids can learn to take care of and display a collection like this without the risk of it losing value, since many bank notes can be found for just a few dollars apiece.

For example, Belarusian notes feature a number of different animals and are available for less than $1 each when found in the right groups. South African currency is great for animal enthusiasts, too, with depictions of everything from lions to oxen. Trains and ships are shown on notes from Costa Rica, Australia and other countries, Johnston explains.

Along with starting him off with his first paper money, Johnston's grandfather took him to a local coin shop in Tucson, Arizona, most Saturdays to check out the "bid board" where he often could buy reasonably priced examples to add to his collection. That time spent together holds special memories for Johnston. The pair also frequented coin shows together, where he got a push of encouragement to become an avid collector. A few more bills that Grandpa picked up at the shows and saved for gifts later made special additions to Johnston's collection.

That was years ago, but that doesn't mean parents and

grandparents don't still encourage kids to collect world bank notes. "We have a number of clients who actively collect with their kids. There seems to be a sweet spot for getting them started," Johnston said, referring to his work with numismatics for Heritage.

That "sweet spot" Johnston has observed most often falls in the age range of 8-12. He sees that as an age where interest can be kindled, just as his was, and cultivated for future growth. And beyond the numerous bank notes available through Heritage,

Numismatic Resources

Coin experts often recommend these resources for kids interested in numismatics as a hobby:

The American Numismatic Association's Young Numismatists Program:

For a nominal yearly fee (depending on the membership level), children aged 5-17 can participate in a wide range of activities sponsored by the American Numismatic Association. This includes participating in the Ancient Coin Project and earning YN dollars that can be spent at monthly online auctions as well as receiving a regular newsletter and other educational resources.

Visit the Young Numismatists section under "Explore" tab at Money.org to learn more about this worthwhile program.

Expert-Recommended Books for Beginners:

A Guide Book of United States Coins by Kenneth

Johnston still suggests coin shows as a resource for adults mentoring youngsters, just as he discovered with his grandfather. He also recommends involving children in the American Numismatic Association (ANA) programs for kids. That's how he took his own interest in collecting to the next level.

The low fee for a yearly Young Numismatists membership is money well spent when it comes to tapping educational resources. Johnston took full advantage of the ANA summer programs with the help of scholarships when he was young. "It

Bressett and R.S. Yoeman (Whitman Publishing)
Standard Catalog of World Coins by Thomas Michael (Krause Publications)

Online resources for researching coin values:

HA.com – Browsing complete auctions sold via Heritage Auctions offers a great resource free of charge.

Numismaster.com – This online resource from Krause Publications shares a wealth of information on both coins and bank notes, including a free newsletter with pricing information. Use the "Find My Coin" and "Find My Currency" features to learn more about your collection.

Apps for Coin Research:

PCGS Photograde – This smartphone app from Professional Coin Grading Services (PCGS) allows users to get help grading coins by placing examples right next to high-resolution photos of United States coins of all ages and denominations.

was great," he said. "I found it to be an incredible way to learn from some of the industry's best."

Johnston points out that a good number of young people veer away from collecting in their teen years but will likely come back to the pastime later in life. Adults should consider hanging on to those early collections during the waning years, knowing that an interest may indeed come full circle later. Collecting buddies are usually happy to get those items back as adults so they can continue to enjoy them, along with the memories they hold.

Johnston certainly proves that inspiring a youngster to collect can lead to a lifetime of learning, not to mention enjoyment. He's still at it as a numismatics professional, and it all started with that gift that kept on giving from a special grandfather.

Chapter 9

COMIC BOOKS AND THEIR ART – COLLECTING FAVORITE CHARACTERS

Generations of American children have grown up reading comic books, and many of those captivated readers have gone on to become passionate collectors. Those with the means will pay good sums to own rare originals along with hand-sketched artwork to go along with their favorites. But believe it or not, there's a place at the comic collecting table for youngsters, too.

Getting a comic book or comic art collection underway can be as easy as taking your collecting buddy to an event referred to by enthusiasts as a "comic con." Such conventions cater to individuals who appreciate comic books, comic art and science fiction media in general, along with a wide variety of related collectibles.

These gatherings of like-minded individuals, some of whom show up in attention-grabbing costumes, are held regularly in major cities across the country. And while they do charge an entrance fee, the experience can be well worth the price when you're cultivating a young collector.

A visit to UpcomingCons.com will connect you with links providing more information on dozens of these events.

" It's pretty easy
to generate
interest when
there's excitement
surrounding
superheroes and
cartoon characters.'
— Jim Steele

Individual comic con pages supply lists of artists who will be in attendance, special guests available for autographs at an additional fee, and other exhibitors including vendors selling comic books and their artwork.

If you hit the booths of dealers specializing in framed original comic art first, however, you might come away with sticker shock. Most of the items they display are hard-to-find originals by major artists, and as you might imagine, they sell for a pretty penny. But high-end sellers usually have a bin or two holding some bargain items as well, where you might find things for $100 or less. Other framed pieces they're marketing will be the type to save up allowance and birthday money to purchase. That doesn't mean you won't find some affordable, or even free, art available if you take in all that the show has to offer.

"I've been to a few comic cons, and indeed have seen original pieces for $100 or more," said Hector Cantu, editorial director for Heritage Auctions. "But some big-time artists have also done sketches in my son's sketchbook for free. Others sell small pieces at their tables for $10 or $15. So it all depends on the artist. Some popular artists might charge a lot; some might do it free; some do it rather reasonably. I guess that's part of the whole collecting game."

One thing to keep in mind is that many sketches done at comic cons are inspired by characters from familiar, and sometimes very famous, comic books. Not all of them, however, are being sketched by the artist who drew the originals, so you may have to insert a bit of discerning guidance here and there where kids are concerned. Nevertheless, the work of these artists can be quite good, even fantastic, and very interesting to those with a penchant for comics.

It can also be great fun for the child to interact with an artist or watch them draw at their table. If the child you're

THE AVENGERS

MARVEL
COMICS
GROUP
12¢

EARTH'S MIGHTIEST SUPER-H

CAN THE COMBINED POWER OF **THE AVENGERS** DEFEAT THE SINISTER SPELLS OF **LOKI, GOD OF EVIL?**

THE AVENGERS... BAH! I'LL DESTROY YOU **ALL!**

SUPER-HEROES!
SUPER-VILLAINS!

Comic book dealers are a great resource for both buying and selling, or simply asking questions.

guiding through the show is fascinated by particular art being produced on the spot, it's age-appropriate and affordable, by all means consider adding it to a collection. You never know when the work of one of the talented individuals at a comic con might go on to become desirable in the future. At the very least, your collecting pal will walk away with something they really like.

Artist Sam de la Rosa, who has inked and finished Spider-Man for Marvel and Batman for DC Comics among other characters, has been participating in comic conventions for more than 30 years and often sketches on the spot for children. His smaller impromptu works sell for as little as $10, and for $30-

Bob Brown and Dick Giordano, *Detective Comics #428*, "The Toughest Cop in Gotham" title page 1 original art (DC, 1972).

Charles Schulz, *Peanuts* Sunday comic strip original art dated 12–23–62 (United Feature Syndicate, 1962).

Dan Spiegle, *Walt Disney Comics Digest* #55 cover original art (Gold Key, 1975).

$50 he'll do a larger drawing – perhaps on a comic book "blank" – which takes a bit more time. He feels these are fair prices so more fans can fit original comic art into their budgets while still making it a worthwhile endeavor for him to pursue.

Kids who approach de la Rosa often request drawings of their favorite characters, especially Spider-Man, and they're very appreciative of the time he spends with them. This includes not only sketching for them but encouraging them to pursue a career in art, if that's their interest. He'll look at original comic art they share with him and gently critique when asked for an opinion. Eager youngsters are usually attending with their families, and some events have special days or times geared especially toward kids, but that wasn't always the case.

"About half the attendees are families now, when years ago it was mostly young men who came to the conventions," de la Rosa said. "Comic book characters are more a part of popular culture these days. Everyone is familiar with the movies based

Ron Frenz and Scott Hanna,
Fantastic Four: World's
Greatest Comics Magazine #
12, Galactus Splash, page 20
original art (Marvel, 2002).

on Marvel and DC characters now, and that helps encourage attendance."

Jim Steele

Jim Steele, chief cataloger for Heritage Auctions' Comics & Comic Art, nurtures his own grandson's interest by encouraging him to read his favorite comic books and to collect those he likes best. "It's pretty easy to generate interest when there's excitement surrounding superheroes and cartoon characters," Steele said.

He's observed over his years in the business that watching artists sketch is a great way to teach kids about how comic books come together, increasing appreciation for the finished product. Steele adds that even the most well-known artists will often sell art prints at shows, and they're willing to autograph them there. These are another affordable alternative for kids with an interest in comic books and their art.

It's also interesting to note that while the sketches of many big-name comic artists sell for tidy sums through Heritage Auctions, others have seen hammer-down prices that even a kid can afford. Work of the late Martin Nodell, who created the Green Lantern; Marvel and DC comic artist Jim Fern; and the late Dave Simons who also worked for the major comic book companies both penciling and inking sketches, have all sold for under $20 at one time or another.

Those are the types of occasional bargain deals found through Heritage Auctions' weekly sales offered online at HA.com, according to Steele. So, even if you're not quite ready to don your Superman cape and venture out to a comic con, you can still find kid- and budget-friendly options for collecting in this genre as close as your own computer.

Jim Steele is chief cataloger for Heritage Auctions' Comics & Comic Art.

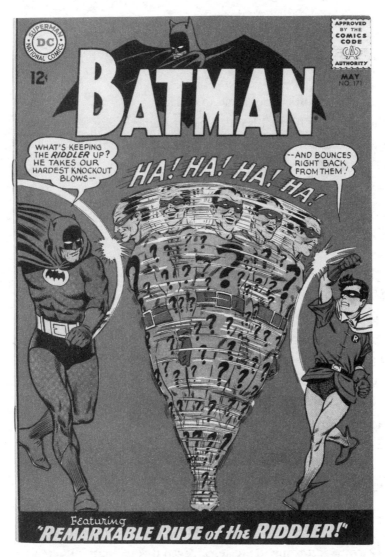

The villian, The Riddler, first appeared in a 1965 DC Comics
issue of Batman, making this Silver Age comic book valuable.

Marvel's The Incredible Hulk debuted in 1962. The great Jack Kirby provided the cover art.

Adolph Hitler was the featured cover villain of this 1941 issue of Captain America, though it was beofre the United States entered World War II.

The first issue of Bone dropped in 1991, introducing the world to Fone Bone, Phoney Bone, Smiley Bone, the Great Red Dragon and Ted.

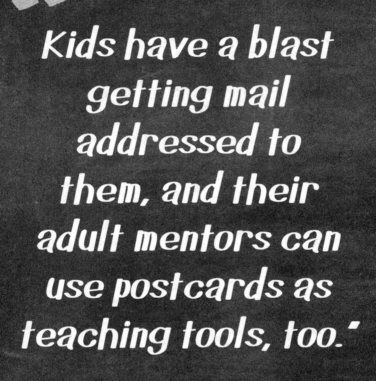

Kids have a blast getting mail addressed to them, and their adult mentors can use postcards as teaching tools, too."

POSTCARDS – DIVING INTO DELTIOLOGY

Summer vacations of yesteryear, long before youngsters had so many online photo-sharing options, often included buying and sending colorful picture postcards. Trips were remembered. Friends and family kept in touch. And collections were launched affordably and simply.

Dede Horan, of Colorado, bought her first picture postcard on the way to Vermont to see her grandparents just before her 10th birthday. "We went across the neatest covered

Two boxes of vintage postcards, mostly travel–related subjects, with various dates ranging from 1905 through the 1950s.
Courtesy of Clars Auction Gallery, www.clars.com

Vintage Thanksgiving and Easter postcards, circa 1910.
Courtesy of Clars Auction Gallery, www.clars.com

bridge and, of course, I had to have a picture postcard of it to remember the trip."

She also lucked into one of the first postcards she added to her fledgling collection when she discovered something stuck between the wall and a faux fireplace mantle in her childhood bedroom. After digging it out with a yardstick, she discovered that it was a really cool cat-themed "squeaker" card from the early 1900s.

More than 50 years and many postcards later, Horan finds herself running the Denver Postcard Show as well as participating in the Denver Postcard Club. Enjoying her hobby as much today as she did way back when, she introduces postcards to youngsters as often as possible.

As a past instructor for a Montessori preschool, Horan

Santa Claus postcard with attached hat with trim and beard made of real hair.
Courtesy of Morphy Auctions, morphyauctions.com

used postcards to teach little ones about faraway lands. She remembers them being a great a tool to spark young imaginations for storytelling, too. At her postcard shows, boxes of bargain cards are kept expressly to encourage beginning collectors. When kids come into her booth, she gives them the chance to take several cards from the box for free.

"Anytime a child or young person expresses interest, I try to encourage that," Horan said. Once they select a few cards, she asks them why they were attracted to those particular choices, to nurture that spark of enthusiasm. Whether they like dinosaurs, sports, animals, or space exploration, there are usually postcards available to fascinate them.

Another collection-building option is to enlist the help of others. Horan's grandparents sent her postcards as they traveled about, and that's still a very viable option to encourage a young postcard enthusiast. Picture postcards can be found in gift shops around the globe, and they're usually inexpensive to buy and send, especially when compared to other souvenir options. Kids can choose a few cards to bring home from family vacations, just as Horan did when she was young.

As suggested on SmartTutor.com, youngsters can also send a brief email to friends and family living in other cities, states and countries requesting a postcard. Kids have a blast getting mail addressed to them, and their adult mentors can use postcards as teaching tools, too.

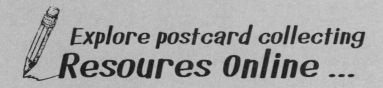

Explore postcard collecting Resoures Online ...

SmartTutor.com – Search for "postcard collection" at afterschool.SmartTutor.com for suggested email wording for requesting postcards from friends and family.

Postcrossing.com – Sign up for a free profile to facilitate sending and receiving postcards from all around the world.

Metropolitan Postcard Club of New York City – MetroPostcard.com – Offers well-researched history, topical categories, and information on postcard artists and publishers.

This postcard depicts the Titanic. It was published by J. Salmon in England and is uncancelled.
Courtesy of Morphy Auctions, morphyauctions.com

Rare Winsch–Schmucker Halloween postcard, unsigned, dated 1913.
Courtesy of Morphy Auctions, morphyauctions.com

As postcards arrive, plotting the location from where they were sent on a map can offer a great geography lesson. A card depicting an interesting landmark or other subject matter can make an intriguing show-and-tell or written report topic in school, too. Looking for postcards from decades gone by reflecting changes in a child's hometown can offer a captivating journey in time, documenting local history frame by frame.

Vintage embossed bluebird postcard, circa 1910.
Courtesy of Clars Auction Gallery, www.clars.com

Challenges can also be a fun way to further a postcard collection. For instance, trying to collect a postcard from every state or seeing how many different postcards can be found featuring a particular kind of animal. Pursuing projects like these make shopping together at antique malls and shows even more fun, and those types of cards often can be picked up very reasonably at a dollar or two apiece, if not less.

As they delve into the world of deltiology, children also learn that collecting postcards can go way beyond the picture variety. Many of the earliest postcards were greetings for holidays ranging from Christmas to Independence Day to Halloween. While not all these cards are affordable, many can be collected for a few dollars each as you peruse antique shops

Four early 20th century Halloween postcards, all with
children themes. Two are Ellen H. Clapsaddle designs.
Courtesy of Conestoga Auction Co., Division of Hess Auction Group,
www.conestogaauction.com

and flea markets together.

If kids want to get serious about collecting in this area,
Marsha Dixey, who works as a consignment director for
Heritage Auctions, suggests looking for examples that are
high in quality, regardless of the age. That means postcards
with no writing or cancellation marks – in other words,
pristine cards that have never been addressed, stamped or sent
through the mail.

Dixey noted that the best examples – which avid collectors
pay the most to own – are very clean in terms of soiling and
stains as well. They do not have creases anywhere on the card,
and the corners are crisp without rounded or frayed edges.

"There are still lots of very nice cards out there to collect

Four Santa in Silk Suit postcards.
Courtesy of Morphy Auctions, morphyauctions.com

that have been mailed or show a bit of wear," Dixey said. She noted that most postcards you'll run across don't fall into that top-notch aficionado category, nor do they have to, in terms of making up a nice childhood collection.

Regardless of the grade, storing postcards with conservation in mind is always a good idea to prevent further damage or deterioration. Dixey suggests hobby shops as resources for storage sleeves specifically sized for postcards. They can also be ordered online doing a quick search for postcard collecting supplies. Hard plastic top-loaders, similar to those used for storing sports cards, afford the most protection from creasing and corner wear. Lighter-weight plastic sleeves will be more affordable, but keep in mind that they don't offer as much security for special collectibles.

Another alternative is organizing postcards in binders. Heavy plastic sleeve inserts that fit into basic ring binders afford both protection and accessibility. These hold four to six cards per page, and make categorizing easy to accomplish.

Binders make postcard storage easy.
Courtesy of Copake Auction, Inc., www.copakeauction.com

Paging through a collection to enjoy it or share with others is a breeze with this setup. After all, part of the fun of amassing a collection is being able to share it with others. Postcards can also be framed for display, either individually or in interesting groupings, using acid-free materials.

So, when exploring ways to entertain the kiddos all year long, don't forget about postcard collecting. Whether old or new, possibilities abound here, and a little stack of postcards could very well lead to a future filled with collecting fun.

This rotating display offers four columns of six double-sided slats for postcard display, 29" high x 11" wide.
Courtesy of Morphy Auctions, morphyauctions.com

"...Parents should guide kids carefully when actually buying online and interacting with other collectors in cyberspace."

Single–signed baseballs are some of the best items to display. Some signatures are difficult to read. This one is recognizable – Albert Pujols.

Chapter 11

SPORTS CARDS AND MEMORABILIA –
BUILDING AN ALL-STAR COLLECTION

It's no secret that the simple act of trading what started as bubble gum cards has grown into a thriving industry over the past few decades. But at the heart of all the big business surrounding the sports card frenzy are lots of kids still enjoying collections as much as their parents and grandparents did years ago. If you have a child in your life

Pennants and pins come in all shapes and sizes. At one time, like the examples pictured above, they came with chocolate! Nearly all stadiums and arenas still offer these at kiosks.

Jacob and Dan Hock pore over Beckett's price guide researching values for cards in their collections. Photo courtesy of Dan Hock

interested in sports, or you want to rekindle your own interest in the hobby, beginning a sports card collection with a youngster can lead to a whole new ballgame.

Dan Hock, owner of Central Coast Sports Cards and Zumer Sport, in San Luis Obispo, California, suggests two key ways to hone a kid's interest in sports card collecting: focusing on types of cards that are "cool" to the individual child, and collecting by region, team or player. But when all is said and done, it's really budget that dictates the best way to go about collecting sports cards.

"Some kids just like the fun of the hobby – searching for interesting or valuable cards, opening new packs – looking for treasures. In any case, how you start a collection is really driven by your budget," Hock said. "Cards come in packs made by sports card manufacturers like Topps, Upper Deck, and Panini.

These packs have sports cards randomly inserted in them – regular cards and special cards called inserts. There are many different kinds of packs – some carry more cards, some feature more inserts, some include an autograph card or a card with a piece of actual memorabilia. The various packs can range from $1 each to $500 each."

Since most people are on a limited budget, Hock suggests starting with the less expensive packs of cards. Buying a variety of affordable packs from different manufacturers lets kids see which type they like best, and then they can discern how they want to build a collection. He notes not only having seen collections based on particular players and teams, but also by state, and even where players went to college as an interesting twist.

Dan's son, Jacob, has been collecting sports cards in earnest since he was 5 or 6. "My dad collected cards when he was young, and then started my collection when I was very young," Jacob said. "I have my own collection separate from my dad now, and we collect different types of cards. I have mine organized by teams I like, as well as by the card's value."

As with most collecting ventures, pulling together a group of sports cards often surrounds the thrill of the hunt.

One of the most popular baseball players currently is Bryce Harper. There are plenty of examples of his cards available, with or without his autograph.

Posters of favorite players remain a fun collectible. Pin it on the wall and no one will forget which team and player you root for.

"I really like the feeling of opening packs and boxes," Jacob said. "I don't know why, but I have always liked that. Buying singles that I specifically need for a team or set is also fun, but opening the packs is better."

Dan Hock notes the main way to further a budding collection is buying packs, as Jacob enjoys, but collectors can also search for individual cards directly.

"If you buy packs, sometimes you can pull a really rare or valuable card. If you prefer to just buy what you need, there are lots of ways to do that, too," Hock remarked. "Many sports card shops have individual cards available by player and by team. Also, many shops carry grab bags, which feature larger quantities of single cards for a low price."

UpperDeck.com suggests that local card shops are the best place to buy cards. Why? The advantage of viewing cards in person, so you can assess the quality and condition of each item, helps with discernment. You also know the cards are authentic when buying from a reputable dealer. Sports card shops sell card holders, binders, and other collecting supplies to help youngsters organize and protect their cards as well. Store owners can also answer questions and guide both children and their collecting mentors as they begin and further collections.

Visiting sports card conventions and shows also provides a way to comparison shop for cards with many different dealers in one convenient venue. Many larger cities host at least one sports card show per year. Attending conventions catering to sports card enthusiasts can also be a great family activity and a way to connect with others interested in sports cards while expanding a collection through buying, selling and trading. Publications like Beckett's *Sports Card Monthly* (order online at BeckettMedia. com.) and online resources including UpperDeck.com provide

One of the biggest sports card shows held annually is the National Sports Collectors Convention. Many card manufacturers, like Panini pictured here, have special cards and giveaways aimed just for kids at this event.

Online resources

recommended by sports collectibles experts

Beckett.com – Beckett offers grading services, forums for collectors, and resources for valuing sports cards as well as publications for sports cards enthusiasts and print-based price guides widely used by collectors.

HA.com – Heritage Auctions provides appraisal services, sports memorabilia auctions, and an online database of prices realized through past auctions, which includes select sports cards.

lists of upcoming shows and conventions across the country.

There are also many online sources for finding specific cards – from auctions to sports card shops to collecting forums. Taking care is paramount when shopping online, however, and some experts suggest getting a good bit of experience under your belt before venturing into the online auction arena. At the very least, parents should guide kids carefully when actually buying online and interacting with other collectors in cyberspace.

When it comes to card collecting pitfalls, unethical dealers top the list. Beware of shop owners who take advantage of kids and new collectors by overcharging and overselling, which translates to convincing them to buy more than they intended. "Being a collector myself, and having a child who collects, I'm very sensitive in this area," Hock said. "Parents should be very careful about finding the right sports card shop. Parents and kids should also educate themselves on counterfeit cards. I personally haven't encountered any, but they do exist."

Setting a budget for collecting also makes sense. Without one,

Signed basketballs are relatively inexpensive and make for a great display piece. Can you guess the signatures on this ball?

Answer: Larry Bird and Magic Johnson.

Numerous shows held across the country offer fans the chance to meet players in person, like Wade Boggs pictured here, to get a signature and a photograph.

it's very easy to become addicted. "I have seen people spend beyond their means," Hock said. "Whether you're an adult or child, if you're going to spend $50 a month, be very careful about turning that into $500 a month."

There are also great sources available for hunting cards online, but take care when buying through web-based venues. Do your homework on price comparisons before visiting online shops. If you decide to take a stab at buying via online auctions, check seller feedback and read the auction details carefully before placing a bid or buying outright.

As you help them along, you'll find that when youngsters discover a passion and take pride in a collection, they naturally want to learn all about their hobby. Older kids usually find that organization and preservation go hand in hand with collecting sports cards. Younger children can learn more rudimentary, albeit important, lessons. "My parents told me reading the players' names helped me to learn to read when I was really young," Jacob Hock said. "I think I know a lot more about different sports and teams because of collecting cards, too."

Kids also learn how to budget and make good buying decisions as young collectors, especially when they have an interested adult guiding them. And, as most parents hope, those lessons can carry over to adulthood.

Take Alison Heath, of Virginia, for example. While she didn't grow up to collect sports cards, what she learned about putting together a collection as a child still guides her today. "When I was a little girl, my dad helped my brother and I amass quite a collection of late 1980s sports cards while he built his collection of late 1950s baseball cards," Heath said.

"Now that I am an adult, I collect mid-century modern furniture and Rosenthal porcelain designed by Bjørn Wiinblad. The patience and persistence my dad taught us by taking us to card shows and dealers, and the discernment we learned in judging quality, definitely helps me in my collecting endeavors today."

Not all kids change direction as they mature, however. Dan Hock's a great example of a collector who grew his hobby into a business later in life. Jacob Hock doesn't see his interest in cards waning anytime soon either. "As far as I know, I will keep collecting them until the companies stop making them," Jacob said. "It's a hobby I've always enjoyed a lot, and I don't think I will ever lose that."

Baseball Memorabilia – Mom Didn't Throw Out the Collection!

Collectors reminiscing about "what ifs" often lament over once-prized childhood possessions kicked to the curb after they left home. Those reflections frequently lead back to a big box of baseball cards Mom couldn't wait to toss. They imagine going through them one by one years later, reliving memories of great Hall of Fame players like Mickey Mantle, Stan Musial, and Willie Mays.

Oh, and then there's what they might have been worth. Don't even get forlorn collectors started on the potential value of their lost treasures.

But if you're a lucky guy like Jeff Figler, who grew up to be a bona fide sports memorabilia expert, you can count rediscovering a baseball card collection as one of the fortuitous turns in your life.

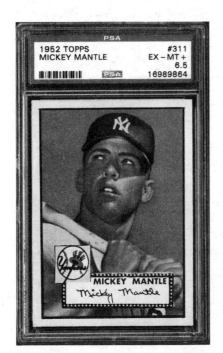

Figler jokingly shared that his mother, Millie, now in her late 90s, would tell you she had a premonition way back when that those cards, along with the numerous comic books she happened to save, would be valuable one day. "In reality,

One of the most recognized baseball cards ever produced is the 1952 Topps card of Mickey Mantle. Even if a dog chewed on it, people will still pay money for an example.

Signed bats can be difficult to display, but they are great for collections. Store model bats aren't too expensive and the signatures really pop on the barrel.

there were bags of cards, and I think she just never got around to throwing them out," Figler said.

By the time his collections resurfaced, Figler's own son was 7 or 8, and the excitement began all over again. Together, they perused the cards, procured price guides and enjoyed figuring out how much each of them was worth. The value of some of the rare examples, however, never exceeded the good times they had together studying those old collections and starting new ones.

Figler's son, now in his late 20s, still has an interest in football memorabilia. When he was young, the collecting duo went to trade shows looking for things of interest while thoroughly relishing the time they spent together.

Recalling those good times makes Figler think back to how his own father helped him get started collecting in his hometown of St. Louis. Even as a kid, good fortune came his way when his dad got to know a number of baseball players through his work in a specialty men's clothing shop. His favorite players on the Cardinals would come in and share an autograph or other memorabilia with Figler's dad while he outfitted them with a new suit.

The personal contacts didn't stop there, though. Figler's dad encouraged his hobby in numerous ways, including helping him write letters to favorite players. Together, they'd wait excitedly for those team members to send back a reply, often with a nifty signed photo. "The key was doing things with my father as he tried to make sure that we did some of that collecting together," Figler recalled.

With both parents and kids leading busy lives today, it's hard to make time for something new to add to the mix. Figler suggests making it a priority, just like his dad did with him. "The main thing is to collect what interests you the most. Spending a certain amount of dedicated time together each week on that focused collecting is a good way to grow a hobby.

Ken Griffey Jr.

Ken Griffey Jr. entered the Baseball Hall of Fame in 2016. Here is perhaps the most recognized card in modern history. Griffey Jr.'s rookie card kicked off the mass production bonanza in 1989. Right: Mickey Mantle bobblehead, circa 1990s, issued by the "SAM" company.
Courtesy of Heritage Auctions, ha.com

You can also learn to work within your budget," Figler said.

He encourages young collectors to send old-fashioned hand-written letters to players if they're really inspired by them, though that method of collecting baseball memorabilia is decidedly not as common as it was decades ago. Players now know their autographs have the potential to become valuable over time, so they frequently charge a fee for signing a photo or ball at sports shows. That doesn't mean getting a signature is beyond a kid's budget, though.

"Most players are not superstars, so autographs might be $10-$20 each," Figler said. At that price, saving allowance or chore money to visit a sports show with an adult mentor can easily lead to bringing home a collectible for many youngsters. Attending a spring training game of a favorite team, if that's feasible, also offers an opportunity to get photos or baseballs signed by favorite players.

In his book *Picker's Pocket Guide to Baseball Memorabilia* (Krause Publications), Figler asserts that both new and old baseball cards are still a great option for starting a collection. They hit their peak of popularity in the late 1990s and early 2000s when values were going through the roof. But Figler notes that even though they haven't bounced back in price to those top levels, baseball cards are still around and as neat to collect as ever. Complete sets are available each year, as well as individual packs. Once the packs are open, the cards are often sold individually, and quite affordably, at shows.

Kids can still have a great time trading cards with their friends, too, just as Figler did when he was young. Buddies on little league teams can trade cards with one another, and there are even online forums for trading sports cards that can be useful with the guidance of an adult. Trading cards is also a great way to narrow a child's focus so that collections are more manageable.

"If you don't focus on teams and players that interest you the most, you end up getting burned out," Figler said. "The sheer volume of memorabilia available today can be overwhelming."

So what else is available beyond photos, cards, and baseballs? In his book, teaching "how to pick like a pro," Figler includes chapters on many different types of baseball memorabilia that might appeal to a kid. From bobble head dolls and statues to pennants and posters, the book covers all the major categories, along with a few fun things young enthusiasts might overlook, like jewelry and board games. This pocket-sized wish book with tips for collecting focuses on everything from dream-find rarities to reasonably priced lots previously sold through various sources.

It's also interesting that "a tangible connection to one's childhood" is at the top of Figler's list for motivations to collect baseball memorabilia. "I listed the connection to childhood first because after interviewing scores of collectors over the years, that's the dominant theme that comes up time and again," Figler said in the book.

Jeff Figler

So even if Mom didn't save your baseball cards, it's never too late to start another collection. Just don't forget to follow Figler's lead and encourage a young person to join you in your collecting pursuits. You'll be singing "Take Me Out to the Ballgame" together in no time.

Sports memorabilia expert Jeff Figler.

ROCKS, GEMS AND MINERALS –
GROWING PEBBLE PUPS
INTO ROCK HOUNDS

Looking for a low- to no-cost collection you can share with a youngster? Don't overlook rock collecting. Children of all ages find fascination in the colors, shapes and textures of rocks, and they can be found virtually everywhere. But can picking up rocks here and there lead to a really rewarding hobby? You bet!

Kids can expand collections to include gems, minerals, fossils and more with a little help from a collecting mentor,

Polished Agua Nueva agate, Mexico.

Jackson Coop and Mackenzie Coop with free-form fossil fish mural

too. That next step often means an adult gifting a kid with a book like *Collecting Rocks, Gems and Minerals, 3rd Edition* (Krause Publications) by Patti Polk to help curious kiddos along. The fascinating array in this guide will most certainly grow the wish lists of young collectors as well as educate them about what they're collecting.

That's how Craig Kissick, director of Nature & Science for Heritage Auctions, got his start. His grandfather took notice of his interest in geology when he was about 9 years old and gifted him with an intriguing piece of purple fluorite along with a great book about rock collecting. Over the following decades his interest grew from a cool hobby into a rewarding career surrounded by things that continually fascinate him.

"It's really more like a calling," Kissick admits of his love for rocks, minerals and the like, and it all started with that one special book inscribed by his grandfather. Now he's a full-fledged "fossil guy" with a keen interest in paleontology, and he still looks forward to his next dig after all these years.

Speaking of digs, Polk shares in her text, "There are basically

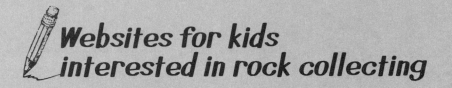

Websites for kids interested in rock collecting

Kids Love Rocks – kidsloverocks.com

This is a great resource for kids interested in starting a rock and mineral collection. Includes activities and projects for free while others, including the opportunity to earn patches for learning about rocks and minerals, that are fee-based.

Rocksforkids.com

Young rock collectors find out how rocks are formed and get help identifying a number of different examples on this site free of charge. Basic information about the hobby will also come in handy for children just getting started.

Smithsonian Kids – smithsonianeducation.org/ students/smithsonian_kids_collecting/main.html

Click on Amazing Collections to learn more about rocks and minerals held in the Smithsonian collection. Sections offering guidance on starting and caring for a collection are also perfect for newbie pebble pups.

two main ways to obtain rocks and minerals: either by going into the field and hand collecting them or by purchasing them from a source such as an Internet dealer, a rock shop, a yard or estate sale, or a gem and mineral show." She also notes that each option employs different strategies.

If hunting rocks in the field sounds like it might be entertaining for you and your young collecting pal, Polk suggests joining a related club in your area to find out the best places to forage. Many clubs have monthly field trips that offer not only guidance on where to hunt, but the opportunity to learn identification and collecting techniques from seasoned pros.

That's how Polk rekindled her interest as a rock hound in her 40s after taking a hiatus from the hobby. She picked up her first rocks when she was about 8 or 9 while hiking in the Las Vegas desert with her dad. One of her intriguing finds was a fossilized shell at the top of a hill, and she couldn't help but wonder how it got there. She went on to find what is known as an Apache tear made of obsidian along with other cool things on those treks.

"It's very common

Milky quartz with copper inclusions, Arizona, 2" x 2".

Lake Superior agate, Michigan, 2" x 1-1/2".

Take Rock Collecting Safety Seriously

In *Collecting Rocks, Gems and Minerals, 3rd Edition*, author Patti Polk offers these important safety guidelines for hunting rocks and minerals in the field:

- Never go alone! Always let someone know where you will be.

- Never enter open mineshafts or adits.

- What is the difficulty of the terrain? What will the weather be like? Are you prepared? Do you have enough food and water in case of emergency? Is your vehicle in good operating condition? Do you have a spare tire?

- Know the status of the land you're collecting on. Is it public or private land? If it is private, you must get permission to enter.

- Don't litter or leave open digging holes, and close all gates behind you.

- Know your limitations and don't ever take any unnecessary risks. No rock is worth it.

Quartz crystal cluster, Arkansas, 3" x 2-3/4".

Dinosaur track.

*Rough flame agate,
Arizona, 3-1/2" x 1-3/4".*

Aden Cornelison is introduced to the monstrous world of fossil collecting by Craig Kissick, Director of Nature & Science at Heritage Auctions.
Photos courtesy Michael Napier

for rock hounds to get back into it as adults," said Polk. Once she connected with a rock club, she was off and running again. She's seen many kids, or pebble pups as the grown-up rock enthusiasts reference them, join the fun in club activities.

Getting kids involved in a rock collecting club also gives them the chance to learn how to polish rocks and use them in jewelry-making or craft projects. They enjoy workshops that focus on geology, how to identify various types of minerals and gems, tools required for rock collecting, and, of course, the all-important issue of safety. And experiencing the field trips sponsored by rock clubs is a great way to learn to respect the natural landscape along with all the plants and animals that go along with that. But how young is too young for rock hunting in the field?

"About 7 or 8 is the minimum in safe areas. There are some

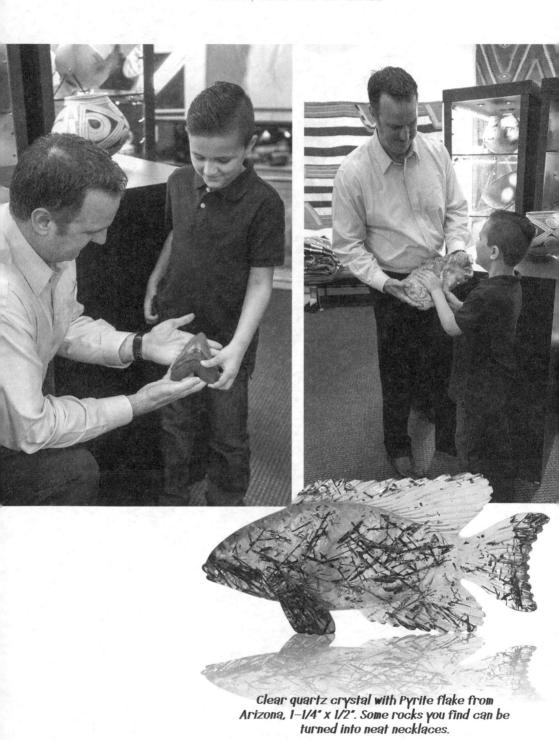

Clear quartz crystal with Pyrite flake from Arizona, 1-1/4" x 1/2". Some rocks you find can be turned into neat necklaces.

This allosaurus dinosaur was discovered virtually complete, articulated and beautifully preserved near the foothills of the Big Horn Mountains in Ten Sleep, Wyoming, in 2007.

This huge Triceratops skull is 7–1/2–feet long, making it one of the largest of its kind. It was discovered on a Montana ranch in 2008.

places that are more difficult to navigate than others," Polk said. Making sure kids are mature enough to take instruction to heart, knowing that there can be dangers in the form of treacherous terrain and poisonous critters to watch out for is vital. When she was a trail guide in Arizona, many families came along on her rock-focused tours, so younger collectors shouldn't be steered away from field trips although keeping safety concerns in mind is wise.

It's not always possible to get budding pebble pups out on forays into the wild, though. That doesn't mean they can't enjoy collecting gems and minerals just the same. "If you just can't for whatever reason, the next best thing is to go to a show," Polk said.

"Varied fossils, sharks teeth, and dinosuar bone fall into the category of rock and mineral collecting."

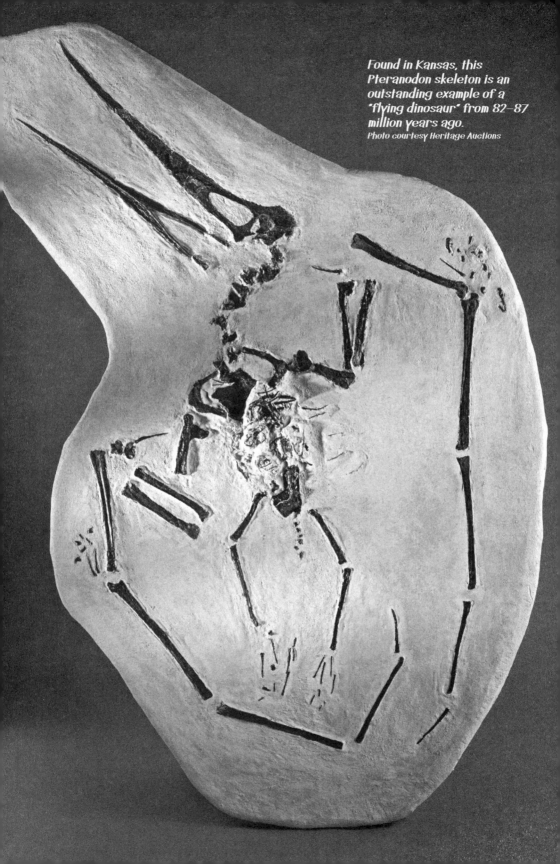

Found in Kansas, this Pteranodon skeleton is an outstanding example of a "flying dinosaur" from 82–87 million years ago.
Photo courtesy Heritage Auctions

Just about every type of rock and stone out there can be found at gem and mineral shows, and most dealers have a basket of crystals or polished rocks selling for $1 or less apiece, perfect for kids. Picking up a sample card that shows a dozen or so different examples of minerals while you're there can serve as an excellent educational tool as well.

Kissick added, "I still like the old rock shop. I'd dig down in an old shoe box under a table to get a rock I liked when I was a kid." Old school shops like that still offer some great bargains for beginners. He also notes that occasionally mineral specimens will go for bargain prices in Heritage's weekly online auctions. While these might not be kid-friendly in terms of budget, they are certainly well within reach of an adult looking to find "the greatest gift a kid's ever going to get."

No matter where you're rock hunting, just be sure to guide a child to bring home only the examples they like the best, otherwise you'll end up with a big pile of unidentified rocks rather than a collection. "It's a process over time. You do have to become more discerning as your collection grows," Polk advised.

While most kids start out just picking up pretty rocks that interest them, there are many ways to hone a collection. Selecting shapes like perfect rounds or hearts, for instance, can provide some focus. Or perhaps certain colors they find appealing can be explored in all their varieties. Other kids collect specific types of minerals or stones such as an array of agates or quartz crystals.

Then there are varied fossils, shark's teeth, and small bits of dinosaur bone that fall into the category of rock and mineral collecting as well. All of these focused areas not only encourage collecting, but learning about earth history and science as each specimen is researched. Kissick encourages visiting natural history museums with your collecting pal as a learning

Author Patti Polk and Kevin Kessler.

opportunity, too, just as he did with his grandpa when he was a youngster.

So if a child you know has a curiosity about natural science, or even a mild interest in picking up interesting rocks, now might be the right time to nudge them along. Those simple stones could lead them down a mesmerizing path filled with collecting amusement right into adulthood.

Chapter 13

STAMPS – THE FUN OF PHILATELY

President Franklin D. Roosevelt, actor James Earl Jones, and tennis star Maria Sharapova – these high-profile public figures, along with many others, have enjoyed the hobby of stamp collecting.

Discovering the fun, history, and artistry associated with stamp collecting, more formally known as philately, isn't just for the rich and famous, though. Anyone can be a philatelist, and that includes the youngsters in your life.

Amy Nicklaus, former executive director for the American Stamp Dealers Association (ASDA), has presented

Booklet of 2004 Spring Flower stamps.

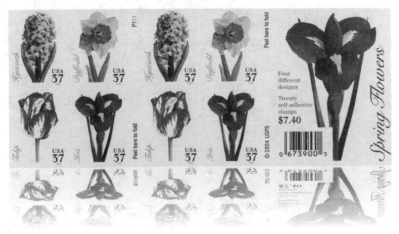

Oops! Value Flies High for Rare Stamp

Arguably the most famous stamp in the world should never have been. But today this upside-down blunder is worth close to $1 million.

Nicknamed by collectors as "Inverted Jenny", the 24-cent blue-and-red stamp was first issued in May 1918 to

stamp collecting as a time-honored tradition for families. She's also noted the encouraging trend of parents bringing the hobby back into the home. In fact, the ASDA mounted a campaign several years ago called The StampLove. The program brought in new collectors to the shows sponsored by the organization, including lots of people who had never thought of collecting stamps previously.

"It's about the hunt – about the joy of finding something that completes a collection," Nicklaus said. "But we have a lot of kids that come into the shows with their parents now. Parents who used to collect are getting back into it with their families."

salute the beginning of mail delivery by air. The valuable error stamp features an image of a Curtiss Jenny JN-4HM biplane – known as a "Jenny" – upside down.

Only 100 Inverted Jenny stamps are known to exist, making them not only rare but quite valuable. A single Inverted Jenny was sold at auction in November 2007 for $977,500. A block of four Inverted Jennys was sold in October 2005 for $2.7 million.

To honor stamp collecting, the United States Postal Service in 2013 issued a souvenir sheet showing six examples of the stamp for $2 each.

Famous in the philatelic world, Inverted Jennys have also seeped into pop culture. In one episode of "The Simpsons", Homer finds a sheet of the stamps – along with a Stradivarius violin and an original copy of the Declaration of Independence – but he doesn't recognize the value of his find and dismisses them. Doh!

2001 Porky Pig stamp.

2007 Star Wars
Darth Vader stamp.

The ASDA is made up of individuals who market stamps, but they are also collectors who want their children and grandchildren to carry on their legacy. Or, at the very least, they want them to know something about a hobby that has been important to them for most of their lives, just like so many other collectors.

"I would also tell parents and mentors that you have to speak in a simple way to get kids involved," Nicklaus added. "How can you expect someone to be interested in something they can't even spell or pronounce? Refer to it as stamp collecting instead of philately to begin with."

Lyle Boardman, secretary and treasurer for the Texas Philatelic Association, has been collecting stamps for more than 60 years. He started as a child with the help of his grandmother, who gave him his first stamps. He has also observed a shift in interest recently through his involvement on the local level in a club for philatelists in central Texas.

"What we have noticed recently are collectors over 40 who are rekindling an interest. They had been exposed to collecting when they were children" and are now getting back into the hobby after finishing school, establishing careers and starting a family, Boardman said.

Like Nicklaus, Boardman encourages attending stamp shows on the local and regional level to learn about philately. And, while attending a stamp show together is a great place to start, Boardman also knows that cultivating interest in a young philatelist will probably take a bit more effort than that.

As with so many types of collections, it's important to look at the interests of the child when you're helping them get started. Try to focus on what they like, and provide them with those first stamps to kindle desire for the hobby.

"Usually, there's something they're already interested in like baseball, Walt Disney movies or even an animal-related theme

like tropical fish. There are Harry Potter stamps out there, too," shared Boardman, regarding guiding young collectors. "They can group stamps together by country or catalog them in albums as topicals or thematics, according to their interests."

Having so many different types of stamps to investigate together adds to the amusement of starting such a collection. In fact, there's a good chance a mentor will find a stamp category relating to one or more of their own interests, making stamp collecting a perfect hobby for adults to pursue alongside the children in their lives.

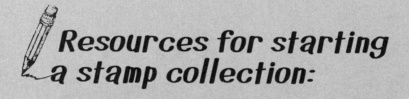

Resources for starting a stamp collection:

American Philatelic Society Youth Programs
Find free and low-cost youth programs through the American Philatelic Society. Go to Stamps.org and click on "Young Philatelists" at the bottom of the page.

Boy Scouts of America Stamp Collecting Badge
Learn more about earning a Boy Scouts stamp collecting merit badge: Search for "stamp" at scouting.org

When adults and children research stamps as a collecting team, they find many facets of the hobby to share and opportunities to learn. Each stamp is a miniature work of art, especially examples that began as engravings. The artistry and events depicted on stamps from around the world can encourage learning about other cultures, geography and history as well.

"Another big aspect of stamp collecting these days is the study of postal history," Boardman said. "If there are other markings on the envelopes indicating how the letter was processed or forwarded, don't just rip the stamp off. Save the whole cover."

A "cover" refers to an envelope or letter that has made its way through the mail system and will usually have cancelled stamps attached. Covers are collected in many different ways, including the popular "first day" covers. These feature a stamp cancelled on its first day of use. But there are also air mail covers, special delivery covers and military-related covers, along with a number of others. There are even covers before stamps were first used in the mid-1800s showing postage due. These are very collectible too, according to Boardman.

Benjamin Franklin one–cent stamp.

Philately, like most collecting pursuits, has its highs and lows when it comes to how much you

George Washington two–cent stamp.

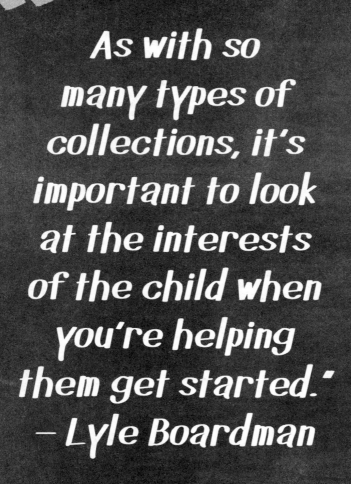

As with so many types of collections, it's important to look at the interests of the child when you're helping them get started."
— Lyle Boardman

1998 Uncle Sam stamp.

can spend. Sure, there are rarities that come on the market costing hundreds, even thousands of dollars, and many people think of these high-dollar examples when it comes to stamp collecting. Veteran philatelists will pay top sums to add those to a collection. That's not all the hobby has to offer, however. Collecting low-cost stamps can be just as fun for a kid, and there's always the possibility the stamps will increase in value over time.

Looking at topics of historical interest, take space exploration as an example, can offer lots of affordable collecting prospects. Many United States stamps have been issued with space and astronaut themes, and Russia has issued hundreds of historical space-related stamps as well. Heritage Auctions has sold space-related first day covers in the past for as little as $14 each, so these types of themed collections can be affordable for beginners.

What's even better? You can actually get started with little or no cash outlay even before you think about purchasing stamps to build a collection. Like Boardman when he was a boy, kids and their mentors can ask friends, neighbors and family members to save for them interesting stamps they run across.

Think about finding a local stamp club and taking a child to a meeting. Adult members of these organizations often give stamps to children in attendance to encourage their interest. On its website, the American Philatelic Society has a number of free and low-cost resources geared toward young collectors, and stamp collecting kits that include an album and starter stamps make a super low-cost gift for a youngster.

Picking With the Pros

There's nothing like learning from the pros, and each chapter in this book is filled with them. Folks who live and breathe their interests make the best educators, whether they're writing articles and books on their topics of expertise, hosting television shows or buying and selling the collectibles of their choice day in and day out.

Here we tap into four very unique perspectives, further illustrating that starting a collection can be enjoyable, rewarding, and might even lead to a lucrative career. Each of these pros started young and has taken his or her pursuits to new heights in different and exciting ways.

Chapter 14

BARBARA CREWS –
COLLECTIBLES EXPERT ENCOURAGES FAMILY FUN THROUGH COLLECTING

Barbara Crews, former collectibles expert for About.com, occasionally shared her views on collecting with kids while wearing her writer's hat. But when it comes to walking the walk, no one has done it better. Crews understands how to recognize and nurture a potential collector and when to back off and stop "agonizing over it." She's also had lots of laughs in the process.

Crews sees collecting as a pastime that can bring families

Barbara Crews and her grandson, Eli, with his LEGO minifigure collection.

Mint-in-box toys command top dollar.

A Star Wars Tauntaun.

*An Imperial All Terrain
Armored Transport
from Kenner, 1981.*

This construction set recreates the iconic Simpsons family house in LEGO form. LEGO sets have increased dramatically in value over the last several years.

together, teach values, and further a worthwhile hobby she hopes others will enjoy, too. When asked for some pointers based on what she's learned from her own experience, especially when it came to guiding her son and grandson, she was pleased to point folks in the right direction.

What kinds of things have you collected with your grandson?

Eli and I have had loads of fun collecting together. Our interests are different, but I do feed his habit by looking for and helping him purchase vintage items that go with his collections, like LEGO mini-figures. In the past, he loved vintage windup toys, Toy Story characters, and old and new vintage Star Wars characters. He still has all of those. He goes with me to the flea market and the occasional antiques store. We frequent one store some friends of

"

Make suggestions
but don't get
upset if they don't
follow those ideas.
See what they're
interested in
and move in that
direction."
— Barbara Crews

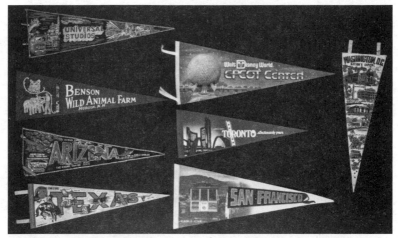

Souvenir travel pennants are a good way to encourage collecting.
Courtesy of Material Culture, www.materialculture.com

mine operate that sells items he finds interesting. He refers to it as the store "where the people like us." He loves to go there with me.

What's the best way to introduce a child to collecting?

Show them things they might be interested in when out shopping or looking around together. That might range from comic books to sports memorabilia to vintage dolls, but let them make the final choice. Make suggestions but don't get upset if they don't follow those ideas. See what they're interested in and move in that direction.

A family vacation is always a good place to start, too. Suggest something that might remind them of the vacation, such as shells from the beach, rocks from the park or something from each stop:

Vintage Marx lithographed metal dollhouse with plastic dollhouse furniture.
Courtesy of Greenwich Auctions, www.greenwichauction.net

postcards, souvenir magnets, or even tacky plastic snow domes from the gift shop. As an added bonus, if they look for snow domes or other collectibles on vacations, it makes gift shop browsing go much easier as they zero in on those special items.

Another tip I used with my son was to give to him a set amount of cash when we went to the flea market together. He really milked that five bucks until the end and learned how to work the sellers to give him a better price, especially since he had a limited amount to spend.

Has there ever been an instance when you weren't successful in planting the collecting seed?

I really think my son would be a full-fledged collector if he didn't live in a small Brooklyn brownstone apartment now. But when I tried to interest my stepdaughter, nothing would click. I finally decided she was just not a collector, especially after we gave her a miniature dollhouse filled with old and handmade treasures. A while later when we asked about it, she said she couldn't remember what happened to it and thought she gave it away. I give her personal stuff now rather than collectibles. She's happier and I'm not agonizing over it.

How are kids who collect different from other children?

I like to think they are more organized, first of all. I also think they're more conscientious about money and the general cost of items.

Quick Draw
McGraw Airplane
Friction Toy, 1963.

Two "Toy Story" plush dolls: Adventure Buddy Buzz Lightyear and Adventure Buddy Woody, each in its original box.
Courtesy of Keystone Auctions, LLC, auctionsbykeystone.com

Disney Toy Story Buzz Lightyear Ultimate Talking Action Figure, Thinkway Toys, 1995.
Courtesy Carden Family Auction Services, www.cardenauction.com

They know how many weeks' worth of allowance needs to be saved to purchase that Holy Grail item they want. My grandson and son might have moved on from previous collections, but they never really got rid of them. They usually culled the best and sold the rest, which *also teaches them the value of money. If they can only sell one of their collectibles at a garage sale for a buck and it cost them $10, they're sure to remember that the next time they buy something.*

Eli can also tell you how long it takes for something to ship from different parts of the country. Now, that's not a necessary life skill, but it was funny to hear a 6-year-old calculate shipping times. I also like to think collecting kids are smarter about computers and utilizing search engines to find stuff they're interested in online.

In the high-tech age, what are good strategies for developing the collecting instinct?

The computer is an excellent way for kids to develop the collecting instinct. They can learn to research what was produced, when it was produced, how much they should spend and rarity. In the case of my grandson, I taught him right. Or maybe as his mom would say, I've created a monster.

When he was first interested in something, we would look on the computer to see what "else" there was. Toy Story comes to mind again. He loved Buzz Lightyear and we would want to see what variations there were and how many might be in a new set that came out. After we figured it out, off we would go on the computer to find those elusive variations or perhaps to see what was available in other countries. The computer is a bonanza when looking for things that aren't sold new locally. Now, with smart phones, it's taken it a bit further. We can search for values when we're actually at the flea market or in a shop.

How does collecting together benefit a family?

Woe is the family that has one collector and the others follow the minimalist theory! But usually that doesn't happen, and collecting can certainly benefit the family that likes to do things together. When my son was younger, we would flea market and

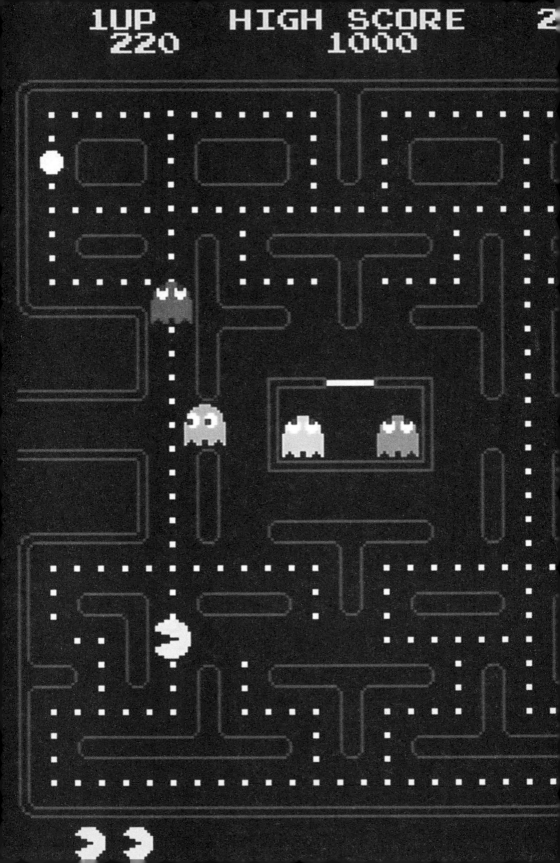

garage sale shop together. Although he would be looking for the stuff he liked to collect, he was also very aware of my interests and would point out an item hidden under the table or in a box that I might not see. It's also great that you absolutely know what to buy them for birthdays and other gift-giving occasions.

What if a child's interests are vastly different from the adult collector's?

A child's collection is the same as an adult's in that it has to speak to them. As far as my family goes, I'm just happy that some of them wanted to collect something. And although they may not want to inherit my 2,000-piece cookie jar collection, they are aware of the length it took to collect those jars and their values. I guarantee that if you have a child who is a collector, you don't have to worry about your valued collection being tossed in the trash when you die. They might not want to keep it, but they'll figure out something worthwhile to do with it.

The original arcade game Pac-Man was introduced in 1980. Since then the Pac-Man character has been featured in cartoons and toys.

"...to teach the importance of being respectful, have a child ask for permission before touching collectibles or sitting on old furniture."
— Cari Cucksey

Chapter 15

CARI CUCKSEY:
ESTATE SALE MAVEN SAYS THEY'RE NEVER TOO YOUNG TO COLLECT

Cari Cucksey, who starred in her own HGTV show "Cash & Cari," is a self-proclaimed "Antiques Matchmaker." She believes "everything was once worth something to somebody, and it can be again" through her businesses, RePurpose Estate Services and the RePurpose Shop in Holly, Michigan. In her early 40s with more than a decade of estate liquidation experience and trash-to-treasure rehab behind her, how did she learn so much about antiques and collectibles? The answer is simple: She started young.

An HGTV bio pegs Cucksey as a buyer, seller, and trader of old stuff from the age of 12, but her passion for amassing things of interest started even before that, when she was first drawn to coins and stamps.

"My grandfather would drag me around shopping with him, and I went with my mother to flea markets and auctions. My father was an influence as well. He had a great workshop and was always bringing things back to life," Cucksey said.

Cucksey started out with coins not only because they were fascinating to learn about but because her dad told her that they

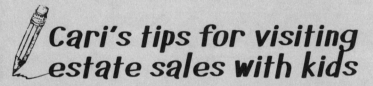

Cari's tips for visiting estate sales with kids

- Don't be afraid to bring a child to an estate sale, but do be prepared to supervise them while shopping.

- Encourage children to look but not touch and to always ask permission before sitting on furniture being offered for sale.

- Teach the importance of being an "antique detective" to look for flaws in items before making a purchase.

- Use the visit as a learning opportunity. Answer a child's questions to teach them about the history and craftsmanship of items they find interesting.

- Remember that teens often find cool items at estate sales, too. Encourage them to go along with you.

Pair of Holly Hobbie embroidery works in blue and purple.
Courtesy of Manor Auctions,
www.manorauctions.com

would always be worth at least their face value, and that made good sense even at a young age. She also collected Garfield and Holly Hobby items and other things that were popular when she was a youngster, proving that nurturing the passion of a wee collector doesn't have to be complicated or expensive.

Now, Cucksey has very eclectic taste when it comes to what she keeps for herself. Her stash ranges from Fiesta dishes she uses every day to varied vintage pottery pieces and even "funky" kitchen implements. "I tend to keep those items I'm not going to see again for a very long time," she said.

Acknowledging she probably wouldn't be where she is today without her childhood collecting adventures, Cucksey believes it's never too young to start. She's convinced the earlier children are introduced to the fun, the more likely they'll take up the hobby in earnest at some point in their lives. "I love it when people bring kids to my estate sales," she said. "Not as many come as I would like, but I do see a lot more people bringing their kids along for the ride now."

What's so hip about taking kids to estate sales? "You get to learn something new every time you go out," Cucksey said. "It teaches them how this old stuff was made and the history behind

PEZ

SPACE GUN

SHOOTS DELICIOUS
PEZ CANDY BULLETS

PACE
GUN

202

49c
LOADED

A PEZ toy Space Gun store display board with six hard plastic original space-themed candy dispensers from the 1950s.

it. And then there's that really cool treasure that hooks them."

Of course, Cucksey suggests following some basic rules when shopping with children at estate sales and other venues where fragile items are being marketed. She encourages teaching early on what to touch and what not to touch. Better yet, to teach the importance of being respectful, have a child ask for permission before touching collectibles or sitting on old furniture. That even goes for handling old toys, which might look like tempting playthings but can easily be broken, not to mention quite costly.

Another valuable lesson to teach youngsters when they're shopping at estate sales is that all purchases are final. That means thoroughly inspecting each item before making a buy to avoid expensive mistakes. "These things have someone else's love. They've been used, so learn to be an antiques detective," Cucksey encouraged.

Show children how to inspect glass and other breakable

Vinyl records remain popular and can be found almost everywhere.

Estate sale treasures can rock the house if you have a keen eye, or ear.

items for chips and cracks. Make sure all parts and pieces are included with games or toys. Look for excessive wear and anything else that might keep an antique or collectible from being categorized as mint or excellent condition. Emphasize that in all but the rarest instances, any issue with condition means paying top dollar isn't a good idea.

Prepared shoppers also know that visiting a restroom just before hitting an estate sale might be necessary to avoid "emergencies," especially if you'll be with a child standing in line waiting to get in. Not all old homes have working bathrooms, and some owners specifically request those areas not be used by customers. With a little forethought, however, you'll do just fine and enjoy your shopping time together.

It's not all about the little ones, though. Teens can have a great time estate sale shopping as well. Cucksey finds her own teenage stepdaughters drawn to vintage clothing and accessories she frequently offers for sale. She often gets requests from others in that age group about collecting "vintage vinyl," what old-timers know as record albums, and eight-track tapes, along with turntables and other old stereo equipment.

Teens are also fascinated by mid-century modern collectibles and home furnishings from the 1950s and '60s, proving the generation gap can indeed be bridged by visiting estate sales together. It just takes a little push in the right direction. Cucksey notes that budget-conscious young adults enjoy looking for household items and decorative accessories for college dorms and first apartments, too.

People who haven't quite defined their passion will ask Cucksey where to start when it comes to collecting at estate sales. "Buy what speaks to you and listen to your gut," she tells them. That goes for guiding children as you shop with them. Find out what interests

Mid–century
enameled copper
jewelry marked
Matisse and Rebajes
1950s horse brooch.
Photos by Jay B. Siegel

them and encourage what fits their age group and budget.

She also suggests visiting a local library with children you're
mentoring to see what books are available on collecting topics.
Just paging through a value guide can spark an interest or give a
child an outlet for learning more about things that intrigue them
the most. Answer their questions thoughtfully, and help them
do further research when appropriate. Hours spent collecting
together will make memories that last a lifetime. They could
even lead to a fantastic career – like Cucksey's.

"...he uses his size to his advantage on occasion to squeeze in and get a better look at the jewelry tables at estate sales."

Chapter 16

CONNOR McCRORY –
A "PICKER PRODIGY"
WHO STARTED AT AGE 6

When it comes to kids and collecting, one clever boy in the Los Angeles area takes the hobby to new heights. Connor McCrory, now quickly approaching his teens, has long made it clear that he prefers scouring flea markets and estate sales over swimming lessons and nature camps. In fact, he received national recognition including television appearances as "America's Youngest Picker" at age 8.

Connor was born with a congenital heart condition that made other traditional activities like sports off-limits for him when he was younger. That didn't stop him from finding and embracing the passion for hunting down items to add to his collections and reselling others. Collecting is the perfect leisure-time activity for an enterprising youngster, and he's zealous about his pursuits.

As you might suspect, Connor's parents are collectors, too. Aime, his mom, started picking up Bakelite jewelry when she was 16, and now Connor helps her add to a growing collection consisting of more than 500 pieces. In fact, one of his favorite finds was a Bakelite bangle he purchased for $25 that is worth about $300. That is, if he decides to sell it – for now it's in Aime's collection.

By quizzing his mom about a box of jewelry he discovered in their home, Connor first learned about Bakelite, a type of plastic used prolifically for jewelry making beginning in the 1930s. He's not shy about teaching others, including adults, how to identify Bakelite now that he's learned the ropes.

But, as Aime explained, Connor's interest in old things

Bakelite jewelry.
Courtesy of Strawser Auctions, www.strawserauctions.com

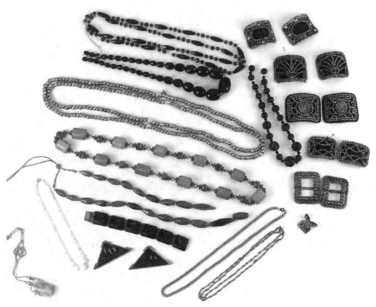

Costume jewelry: 10 marcasite shoe buckles, two coral necklaces, a pair of Bakelite clips and bracelet, an amber–style ethnographic necklace, an agate necklace, three miscellaneous red beaded necklaces, a small white coral necklace, and a long silver–plated bead necklace.
Courtesy of Butterscotch Auctioneers & Appraisers, www.butterscotchauction.com

Connor loves helping his mother add to her bangle collection as well.

Bakelite pins Connor helps his mom collect.

Connor with one of his Lionel trains when he first started collecting.

actually began with model trains a number of years ago. "There's a train store in Burbank we used to visit because he liked Thomas the Tank Engine back then," his mother recalled. "One day he noticed the old trains in the store, and from then on he only wanted those." Now one of Connor's main interests is Lionel trains, and he can rattle off models and their values like any adult with a penchant for vintage toys. And Connor doesn't stop there.

What makes Connor a "picker" in the true sense is that he's also an enterprising young antiques dealer. He sells through online auctions, has a flea market booth that he tends on weekends, and even runs estate sales on occasion. He loves meeting people at the flea market to learn about what they collect and talk shop with other dealers who are repeatedly amazed by him.

When he's not doing the selling, Connor enjoys spending his free time scouring estate sales and shopping online for bargains he can either add to his collections or sell for a profit. "We've taught him to be nice and respectful as he shops alongside adults. He will help and tell people when things are priced too low. That happens pretty often, actually," Aime said. But Connor admits in an online interview with one of his adult mentors,

Martin Willis, a regional sales agent for James D. Julia, Inc., that he uses his size to his advantage on occasion to squeeze in and get a better look at the jewelry tables at estate sales.

How did he amass enough knowledge to do all this at such a young age? That's where the prodigy part of the equation comes into play. "He just has an almost uncanny sense of what's collectible and valuable," his mother said. "It's just been remarkable to watch. And it's amazing that he's found something he's so passionate about so early on."

In true picker prodigy form, Connor retains an inordinate amount of the research he does on his finds. He can talk antiques and collectibles quite amazingly, whether the topic is how Rookwood pottery is marked or the value of Stickley furniture. Unlike many kids his age, he never misses an episode of "Antiques Roadshow" or "American Pickers." He says the shows inspire him and fuel his excitement about his hobby.

When a television producer asked Connor if he would rather own an antiques shop or be on TV, he didn't think twice about his reply. Aime quoted Connor as saying, "Television shows go off the air, but my shop will go on forever, and I can pass it on to my family."

Willis recognizes Connor's potential and plans on following his progress. "I see someone who can become an icon if he never loses the passion," Willis said. "He has the potential for becoming an amazing generalist in this business."

Willis found a fascination with bottle digging when he was just 9 and went on to learn more about antiques through his father's auction company. He feels Connor has a lot to look forward to, whether he follows his dream of owning a shop or decides to work for an auction house. He also encourages Connor and other kids with an interest in antiques and decorative arts to look toward a college education to augment their learning. Possibilities include concentrating on American or European

Connor is also a collector of Barbie dolls. When he was younger he thought they looked like Marilyn Monroe, and he's quite a fan.

history or, perhaps, art history.

Connor actually has many adult mentors who spur him along with information on specific topics. "At first, they might think I'm 'just a kid,' but I'm not," Connor said. "Once they know me, they help me learn a lot more about antiques."

Connor's mom certainly qualifies as one of those helpers. Aime gave him a boost in getting started on eBay, and Connor quickly learned the ins and outs by using completed item listings for research. Aime then introduced her son to selling – both on- and off-line – and watched him soar.

Connor uses sites like Etsy.com and rubylane.com to do research and has a subscription to WorthPoint.com for pricing research. He was an honorary junior "Worthologist" several years ago, with the guidance of Willis. Connor uses books and auction catalogs he's collected as reference materials, too, just like an adult collector.

Aime teaches Connor about the importance of budgeting, profiting and not buying everything in sight. As far as managing his money goes, she added, "He does tend to want to borrow, and it's a fine balance between spending and saving and being able to get what you want. But he's gotten much better," Aime said. "I've been teaching him about investing, and he keeps the profit to reinvest now. We keep his funds in what we call 'the bank of Mommy' to keep an eye on spending."

Miscellaneous costume and gold–filled jewelry.
Courtesy of Kaminski Auctions, www.kaminskiauctions.com

Another aspect of Aime and Connor's collecting relationship is that she learns as much, or more, from him as he does from her. She knew a bit about Bakelite as a long-time collector and was familiar with older Barbie dolls, for instance. But Connor's passion for these things has taken her further than she ever expected. "I just love it. He has taught me so much as he's learning."

During his interview with Willis, Connor said – as all collectors eventually discover – that mistakes are one of the best ways to learn in the antiques trade. "I made one today," Connor said. "I paid $40 for a bracelet, and then I saw one on eBay for $4. No antique dealer knows everything."

With many of the lessons that grown-up collectors and dealers take to heart already committed to his young mind, this extraordinary boy is definitely going to be one to watch as he matures. He's also a great example of what can happen when a collecting spark is recognized in a child and further kindled. You never know when you might discover the next amazing picker prodigy.

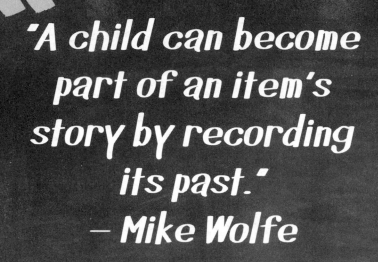

"A child can become part of an item's story by recording its past."
— Mike Wolfe

· Chapter 17 ·

MIKE WOLFE'S
KID PICKERS:
THE NEXT GENERATION
OF TREASURE HUNTERS

Millions of folks around the globe watch as Mike Wolfe and his picking partner Frank Fritz scavenge for artifacts and relics in barns, basements and abandoned buildings, meeting interesting characters along the way. But way before Wolfe imagined he'd be sharing his secrets for hunting down "rusty gold" with his viewers on the History Channel's "American

1900s antique bicycle with spring seat and wire basket.
Courtesy of Scheerer McCulloch Auctioneers,
www.smauctioneers.com

History Channel's "American Pickers" star Mike Wolfe.
Photo courtesy of Mike Wolfe

Gas–powered Indian bicycle with a fully functional two–stroke, 49cc gas–powered engine. It features a working headlight, right hand throttle, and numerous touches constructed from antique bicycle parts to give the impression of a replica of an old Indian motorcycle. The frame and components have been given a patina that looks like rust.
Courtesy of Morphy Auctions, morphyauctions.com

Green glass Denwood & Sons Mineral Water bottle in design of Hiram Codd, 1860, and clear glass Diamond Jubilee flask with original glass ball stopper.
Courtesy of Heritage Auctions, ha.com

A mint–in–box Rancor Monster of Star Wars fame can be worth $275.

Early child's Penny Farthing high–wheel bicycle is constructed from metal with wood handlebars and a replacement wood seat; 39" x 32–1/2" x 14".
Courtesy of Morphy Auctions, morphyauctions.com

Pickers," he was polishing his own picking skills.

Yes, the star of this hit television show looks back with affection on his days as the original "Kid Picker."

"The show has really turned into a family show," Wolfe said. With so many reality television programs focusing on topics inappropriate for kids, he sees families turning to "American Pickers" more and more for entertainment they can enjoy together.

"Children who watch the show share their stories with me, and I find them reminding me of myself at that age. The things

I found back then became my toys through imagination," Wolfe recalled. His first collections included everything from comic books to monster models, like so many kids, but his favorite finds were a number of bicycles destined for the dump. In fact, before he was picking in front the camera, his love for old bicycles led him to own a bike shop.

Remembering all the fun he had picking as a kid encouraged Wolfe to brainstorm about other ways to involve children in collecting hobbies. He sees his book, *Kid Pickers,* co-written with his long-time friend Lily Sprengelmeyer, who also was a picker at a young age, as a "Collecting 101" guide written to appeal to children from 8 to 12 years old.

So what does it take to be a Kid Picker? Picking with prowess at a young age, according to Wolfe, stems from traits children hold inherently. Curiosity, imagination, and the longing for adventure all drive youngsters, and they can rarely resist the draw of a good treasure hunt. "Every child is a collector," Wolfe said. He's seen it not only in the kids who relay picking stories to him,

Kid Pickers: How to Turn Junk Into Treasure.
Photo courtesy of Mike Wolfe

but in his own daughter when she was as young as 3. A picker in the making, she often found interesting things ranging from old bottles to unusually shaped rocks to bring home while she and her father were out on walks together.

Reading *Kid Pickers*, children learn about all kinds of places holding treasures waiting to be found, with sections on garage sales, thrift stores, live auctions, antique shops, and flea markets – basically, all the places that grown-ups would take their collecting buddies to shop for dusty finds.

"The easiest thing is to submerge them by helping to find those places to treasure hunt," Wolfe said about getting kids interested in collecting. The book covers the big three: rarity, condition, and age. Essentially, kids get all the basics for making the best picking choices possible wherever they may be hunting. They learn about getting the best deals, too.

"Understanding the business side of things is important. It instills the value of a dollar," Wolfe said. Remembering back to when he first started his picking pursuits, Wolfe knows that kids generally don't have a lot of money to spend on collections. He sees bargaining as an essential tool to master at a young age in order to make limited cash go further.

Beyond that, Wolfe said, "It's not money driven." In fact, early on, *Kid Pickers* urges readers to "forget about what something's worth or what everyone else around you likes." Creating a unique story and finding the individual passion for collecting become the overarching message throughout the book. Many times that distinctive story comes about by making a connection with a really cool find.

"The best chapter for me was the one on understanding family and community history," Wolfe offered. "When you learn about the related story, that piece comes to life." One way to do that, the book suggests, is asking about the story that goes along with a piece purchased at a neighbor's garage sale, for instance. A child can become part of an item's story by recording its past. That includes documenting the history of family heirlooms passed on to budding collectors.

The book teaches kids and their mentors alike to go beyond

KidPickers.com

As a go-along with the *Kid Pickers* book, Mike Wolfe of "American Pickers" created KidPickers.com, a social network of sorts for children interested in connecting with other young kindred spirits. Youngsters visiting the Kid Pickers Pickin' Post, with the supervision of their parents, can create a profile, share their finds and collections, and tell fun stories about the cool stuff they discover on their picking adventures.

gathering oral history. It encourages using resources like local libraries to tap books on specific collecting topics and researching online to double-check facts and learn more about the history of different types of collectibles.

Another fun addition puts a spunky face on the topic. Vignettes highlighting a number of Kid Pickers are sprinkled through the book. From Chloe Paris, 8, proudly displaying her antique Singer sewing machine, to Austin, 11, who dug up a number of old bottles near his grandfather's shop, kids out there practicing the art of the pick add a relatable touch.

Repurposing and recycling, known as "picking with a purpose," gets a nod in the text, too, along with outfitting kids' rooms with their favorite finds. These concepts actually go quite well together since children can learn to use old objects in new ways, just as adults do. Creative thinking and originality get strong encouragement in this area as the book teaches, "No one ever stood out in a crowd by doing what everyone else was doing."

Basically, all the aspects of "American Pickers" translate into concepts youngsters understand, and when they're finished with the book, they can head online to learn even more and interact with other kindred kids at KidPickers.com.

"We're constantly looking for different ways to teach children," Wolfe said. "American Pickers" has even been converted into a teacher's curriculum. The idea of a cartoon series on Kid Pickers has been tossed around as well.

Why reach that far to get youngsters involved? Wolfe explained, "Kids tell me that I inspire them, but I tell them that they inspire me. Developing these resources for them is one of the most rewarding things I've ever done."